The Williamson Reports: A Study

by
SARAH K. VANN

The Scarecrow Press, Inc.
Metuchen, N.J.   1971

Copyright 1971 by Sarah K. Vann

ISBN 0-8108-0375-5

Library of Congress Catalog Card Number 75-149992

Table of Contents

Chapter		Page
Acknowledgments		iv
Introduction		vii
I.	Background of the Inquiry into Library Training by the Carnegie Corporation	1
II.	Bertram's Memorandum and Further Plans for the Study on Training	42
III.	Williamson and the Preparation of the Report	63
IV.	In Fulfillment of Objective One	103
V.	The Reports of 1921 and 1923	141

Appendices

1.	Statement Prepared for Sarah K. Vann by Dr. Charles C. Williamson, June 1955	178
2.	Extracts from a Letter to Sarah K. Vann from Dr. Charles C. Williamson, May 23, 1955	193
Index		203

Acknowledgments

Data for this study were gathered and analyzed during the preparation of my doctoral dissertation submitted to the Faculty of the Graduate Library School of the University of Chicago and later published under the title, Training for Librarianship Before 1923; Education for Librarianship Prior to the Publication of Williamson's Report on Training for Library Service (Chicago: American Library Association, 1961). For this study, as for my dissertation, I am indebted to all those who gave me advice and counsel, especially to Dr. Lester Asheim, then Dean of the Graduate Library School and recently Director, Office for Library Education, American Library Association.

It is with pleasure that I reiterate my special indebtedness to the following for their contributions:

To Dr. C. C. Williamson for permitting me to use his archival materials relating to his study on Training for Library Services: A Report Prepared for the Carnegie Corporation of New York (New York: 1923). Included in that material was a copy of his original report, "Training for Library Work," prepared for the Carnegie Corporation in 1921, the content of which, upon comparison with that of the 1923 published report, compelled further inquiry. To Dr. Williamson also for preparing a brief autobiographic sketch which is included in the appendix with extracts from a letter from Dr. Williamson expressing some of his recollections concerning the Carnegie study.

To the Carnegie Corporation of New York for permitting the use of documents relative to the Williamson reports and for permission to publish the 1921 report on "Training for Library Work."

Introduction

In 1923 the report on <u>Training for Library Service</u>, prepared by Dr. Charles C. Williamson for the Carnegie Corporation of New York, appeared. It is a report long cited as ending a phase in the history of education for librarianship known as the "Dewey to Williamson" period. And so it may be described. Equally it may be described as marking the end of unsystematized Carnegie contributions to library education and as introducing an era of formalized contributions from the Corporation to such schools as the School of Library Service, Columbia University, and the Graduate Library School, University of Chicago.

Properly also it may be described as being based on an earlier report, "Training for Library Work," prepared originally for the Carnegie Corporation in 1921.[1] The original report fulfilled two objectives: (1) to aid the Corporation in formulating its policies in respect to training for librarianship; (2) to analyze the problems of providing trained personnel and to suggest plans of development in order to improve library service.[2]

When the published report, <u>Training for Library Service</u>, appeared in 1923, it fulfilled--or seemed to fulfill--the second objective only, for all material of a confidential nature was deleted from it. Consequently, divested of specific recommendations to the Corporation and tempered somewhat by the removal of some subjective opinions, the report represented largely one man's opinion both on the problems of training and on the problems of service for small libraries. Prepared, further, without direct consultation with the Committee on Library Training of the American Library Association or with the Association of American Library Schools, the report reflected little awareness of the efforts, oftentimes futile, sometimes partially successful, of those associations to formulate standards of training.

The unpublished report contained no bold, innovative approach to the problem of library training; even its concept of certification was an extension of a plan identified by Williamson in 1919 in his speech, "Some Present-Day Aspects of Library Training." It is to that speech rather than to the report on <u>Training for Library Service</u> that the genesis of the movement resulting in the creation of the Temporary Library Training Board by the American Library Association can be traced. Were it not for the contents of the <u>unpublished</u> report, an appropriate line of demarcation for identifying an epoch of history in library training would have been the creation of that Temporary Board. By that action the Association proclaimed its responsibility for the structuring and accrediting of educational programs and brought to maturity the efforts of the Association to formulate plans for standardization and accreditation.

However, the gift of $10,000 from the Carnegie Corporation to the Temporary Library Training Board on November 22, 1923,[3] and the contribution of $5,000 on the same date for the preparation of textbooks,[4] both fulfilling recommendations made in the <u>unpublished</u> report, magnified the significance of the report for which librarians and library schools had long awaited. While the gifts were fortuitously timed, there seems no doubt but that the recommendations would have been fulfilled or rejected by the Corporation with or without the publication of the report in 1923.

Since, however, the report was published, it seems fitting to survey the events leading to the sponsoring of the study on "Training for Library Work" by the Corporation and to the preparations made for the study by C. C. Williamson, and to examine the content of the 1921 report. The detailed analysis should provide a clearer historical perspective with which to view the origin and purpose of the report about which, in 1931, Louis R. Wilson inquired of the American Library Association, "I want to know, for example, what prompted the Carnegie Corporation to have Williamson make the study."[5]

In response to the inquiry, Anita M. Hostetter, then Executive Assistant of the Board of Education for Librarianship, wrote:

> I have been most interested in tracing the reasons for the Williamson Report and equally disturbed that so little definite information seems to be available in print. [6]

Carl Milam, then Executive Secretary of the American Library Association, replied in a similar tone of uncertainty:

> I can not answer more specifically than Miss Hostetter did your question about the reason for the Williamson investigation of library training ... My assumption is that the Carnegie Trustees, having discontinued the erection of library buildings but having continued their interest in libraries, turned to library training as a possible field of usefulness. This field may have been chosen because some money had been given by Mr. Carnegie and the Corporation to certain library schools. [7]

This study will answer, somewhat belatedly and in part, the inquiry of Louis R. Wilson and others as to what prompted the Corporation to make the study on "Training for Library Work."

ix

Notes

1. Williamson II, p. v. The "Foreword" reads: "The study on which the following report is based." (Italics mine)

2. Williamson, Charles Clarence, "Notes on the Aims, Scope and Method of the Study of Training for Library Service, for Discussion at the Meeting of the Advisory Committee, to be held Wednesday, April 28, 1920." (Typewritten.) p. 3. See p. 56 of this study for the exact text of the two objectives.

3. Robert M. Lester, Review of Grants for Library Interests, 1911-1935 (New York: Carnegie Corporation of New York, 1935), p. 144.

4. Ibid.

5. Letter from Louis Round Wilson, July 14, 1931. (in the files of the American Library Association.)

6. Letter from Anita M. Hostetter, July 17, 1931. (in the files of the American Library Association.)

7. Letter from Carl Milam, July 21, 1931. (in the files of the American Library Association.)

****

Scarecrow Press is making available, simultaneously with the publication of The Williamson Reports: A Study, the texts of Williamson's "Training for Library Work" (1921) and Training for Library Service (1923), both of which were prepared for the Carnegie Corporation of New York.

Bibliographic Note

Throughout this study, in footnotes, and in the index, the following abbreviations are used:

Williamson I   Williamson, Charles Clarence. "Training for Library Work: A Report Prepared for the Carnegie Corporation of New York." Advisory Committee: Herbert Putnam, J.H. Kirkland, [and] Wilson Farrand. New York, 1921.

Williamson II   Williamson, Charles Clarence. Training for Library Service: A Report Prepared for the Carnegie Corporation of New York. New York, 1923.

In footnotes the following abbreviations are used:

LJ   The Library Journal. Vols. 1-50. New York, F. Leypoldt, 1876-78; New York, Publications Office, 1879-1925.

PL   Public Libraries. Vols. 1-28. Chicago, Library Bureau, 1896-1923.

In the index the following abbreviation is used:

"Summary"   Williamson, Charles Clarence. "Summary of Report on Training for Library Work." Prepared for the Carnegie Corporation of New York. 1921.

Chapter I

Background of the Inquiry into Library Training by the Carnegie Corporation

Andrew Carnegie's Developing Interest

In 1905 Andrew Carnegie acknowledged, in an address before the class of the Western Reserve University Library School, that "nowadays professionally trained people [i. e. librarians] are needed."[1] In so doing he was reversing an opinion which he had expressed in 1890 that persons could be found who were naturally adapted to library work.[2] Despite his earlier attitude and the crystallization of his philosophy that

> the city, county and state library authorities, and if not they, the librarians' profession might well take the initiative and to some extent the burden of providing adequate facilities for training librarians.[3]

Carnegie made contributions to four institutions offering, or hoping to offer, some form of library training. These four institutions were: (1) Western Reserve University; (2) the Carnegie Library of Pittsburgh; (3) the Carnegie Library of Atlanta; (4) the New York Public Library.

Having made the contributions, Carnegie and, later, the Carnegie Corporation found it impossible to remain indifferent to the problems of training, and, by 1918, the Corporation considered making an "inquiry into the subject of schools for training librarians."[4] Two studies were made: one, in 1917, before consideration of the inquiry, was

made by Alvin S. Johnson; the second study, directed by
C. C. Williamson, was undertaken as the result of the
resolution in 1918 by the Trustees of the Carnegie Corporation that an inquiry into the subject of schools for training
librarians was being viewed.

Before examining the contents of the two studies
made for the Corporation, a reference to Andrew Carnegie's
early attitude toward library training and his subsequent
contributions to four library training programs will be noted.
Because of the selection by the Corporation of C. C.
Williamson to undertake the inquiry concerning library
training, references will also be made to his association
with two of the library schools which he later surveyed, those
at Western Reserve University and the New York Public
Library.

Carnegie's Refusal to Assist Melvil Dewey in 1890

Melvil Dewey was anxiously determined to insure the
existence of the School of Library Economy which he had
established under precarious conditions at Columbia College
in 1887. Two years later, when he succeeded in transferring the School to the New York State Library, with the
understanding that "no financial liability on the part of the
State be incurred,"[5] he was compelled to seek financial
assistance from those professing interest in library work.
Not least of those who had publicly expressed interest in
libraries was Andrew Carnegie who, in viewing the best
fields for philanthropic efforts, had written in December,
1899:

> The result of my own study of the question, What
> is the best gift which can be given to a community? is that a free library occupies the first
> place, provided the community will accept and

> maintain it as a public institution, as much a part of the city property as its public schools, and, indeed, an adjunct to these.
>
> No millionaire will go far wrong in his search for one of the best forms for use of his surplus who chooses to establish a free library in any community that is willing to maintain and develop it. 6

Encouraged by the pronouncement, Melvil Dewey informed Andrew Carnegie by letter and by visit of the plight of the Library School, and on May 12, 1890, wrote Carnegie:

> I have for many years struggled with my limited means to do what I could for these pupils in the firm belief that some one would feel it a privilege to give us the means to secure needed help. 7

Carnegie, however, despite his philanthropic zeal to further the development of libraries by providing buildings, was not willing to assume a concomitant responsibility in contributing to the training of librarians. After a visit from Dewey he wrote on May 15, 1890:

> Your interesting visit was the first I had ever heard of the school for librarians. I was interested in all you said, but you misunderstood me, if you thought I had made a positive promise to contribute funds. This is a matter which requires much consideration. I have taken occasion to inquire of several parties about the supply of proper persons for libraries, and find that <u>there is no difficulty in getting persons naturally adapted for this work.</u> We employed one for the Braddock's Library who gives entire satisfaction; and Allegheny has got one. In Baltimore, I was told that it was really wonderful how many of their young assistants developed into splendid librarians. (Italics mine). 8

Thus unceremoniously did Andrew Carnegie refuse to offer financial assistance to the New York State Library School. Melvil Dewey, quite unwilling to accept the decision, wrote again informing Carnegie that his information had been secured from persons not well informed. He added that, even while writing the letter, "your librarian at Pittsburg was on his way to ask for just this help which you seem to think is not very important."[9]

Prophetic of what Alvin S. Johnson[10] and C. C. Williamson[11] were to advise much later, Dewey wrote:

> You would accomplish ten-fold more good for your fellow men, in the lines in which you have shown so much interest, by enabling us to train ten to twenty librarians each year, than by building splendid buildings & leaving it to chance as to whether they shall do ten or twenty or fifty or possibly eighty or ninety per cent of the good that is possible.[12]

Continuing his critical comments on buildings without trained personnel, Dewey confessed:

> I feel exactly as a missionary in lower New York ought if he saw the poor people freezing & starving & was given a palatial church but refused a few thousand dollars needed for things vastly more pressing & important. I am sure that as you think of this matter you will come to the conclusion that you have not enjoyed your full privilege nor discharged your full duty by erecting a beautiful building without making sure that it does a work equal to the cost & capacity of the plant. Pray think on this side of the great work & if I can ever be of any service feel free to call upon me.[13]

As if making one final desperate attempt to interest Carnegie in the Library School, Dewey concluded:

> The man who wrote 'Triumphant Democracy' cannot long be kept in ignorance of as great an educational movement as we have in hand & I feel absolute confidence that if your life is spared, we shall yet find one of the warmest friends & supporters of the Library School & that you in turn will find it your most valuable ally in helping the public by means of libraries which are daily coming nearer to their position as the colleges for the people.[14]

Background of the Inquiry   5

Aftermath

The appeal of 1890 was ineffectual; Melvil Dewey's assistance was never sought nor did Andrew Carnegie allocate any funds to the New York State Library School either during Dewey's incumbency or later. It was not until 1926 that the oldest library school received any Carnegie funds; even then, however, the funds were received indirectly through the transfer of the Library School to Columbia University. Before the approval of the transfer had been made by the Regents of the University of the State of New York on April 21, 1926,[15] the Carnegie Corporation, in March of that same year, had assured Columbia University of its intention to contribute, for a period of ten years, $25,000 annually for the support of a library school embodying the New York Public Library School.[16]

Carnegie's Contributions to Library Training

To Western Reserve University, 1903

Thirteen years after Carnegie had refused to provide financial assistance to the New York State Library School, Charles F. Thwing, president of Western Reserve University, announced on February 23, 1903, that Carnegie had made an endowment of $100,000 to aid in the educational program for librarians to be offered at Western Reserve.[17] Library Journal proclaimed the endowment the most important event of the year in the library field, noting that

> The marked increase within the last few years of agencies for instruction in librarianship, through special courses, summer schools, and the like, are indication of an increasing demand, and the only effective means of limiting the influence of superficial and inadequate training

> lies in widening the scope and influence of
> training of the better sort.[18]

The Cleveland Plain Dealer, in commenting on the gift, editorialized:

> It is doubtful whether Mr. Carnegie, with all his gifts for libraries, has ever devoted the same amount of money to such a useful end. In providing ultimately for a trained force of men and women to administer these libraries, he has supplied a want of his own creation.[19]

In thus appraising the endowment, the Plain Dealer repeated unknowingly the reason advanced by Melvil Dewey in 1890 that Carnegie aid in the program of library training.

Background Data on the Establishment of the Library School

The initiative for the establishment of a training program in Ohio of some type had been taken as early as 1900 by the Ohio Library Association. At its meeting of October 3-5, 1900, a detailed survey of what had been done in the state in regard to library training and a review of needs were presented by the Ohio Committee on Library Training.[20] The Committee, composed of W. H. Brett and Electra C. Doren, presented a report showing that every type of training had been considered: the Dayton Public Library Training program, 1896-1898; lectures at the Cleveland Public Library summer programs; pupil assistant training at Ohio State University, Oberlin, and Western Reserve University. The Committee further noted that Ohio had through the years employed 26 graduates of the library schools of New York (State Library School and Pratt Institute) and of Illinois.

Though expressing gratification over the appreciation for library training in the state and acknowledging that in some instances high excellence and efficiency had been attained without training, the Committee recommended a

Background of the Inquiry 7

course in one of the regular library schools to those interested in library work; frankly evaluated the summer school program as inadequate preparation, "its function being to aid those already in library work to reach greater efficiency";[21] and regarded correspondence work as unfeasible unless there were available equipment and a faculty equal to that of the regular library schools.

Following the acceptance of the report the Association approved a resolution

> That the Committee on library training be recognized as one of the standing committees of the association, and that it be instructed to collect information upon the educational and technical requirements for library assistants in the various libraries of Ohio. [22]

An implementing step was taken by Brett who, increasingly concerned over the need for trained personnel in the Cleveland Public Library. Convinced that the need could best be answered by the establishment of a library school,[23] he approached President Thwing of Western Reserve concerning the establishment of a library school at the University. A committee[24] composed of Allen D. Severance, Edward C. Williams, Linda A. Eastman, and Brett,[25] estimated the annual expenses for conducting such a school and detailed the needs of physical equipment. The committee further suggested that the admission requirement and length of course be equal to those of the Albany School but, in addition, enumerated four specific ways wherein the Ohio program would differ from that at Albany, one being the securing of the aid of the university faculty for the advanced courses in bibliography and reference work.[26]

The work of the committee is significant in education for librarianship in that it was the first positive step taken toward fulfilling the prophecies made at the turn of the century that library schools should be connected with universities. More significantly, the report was received favorably by the Trustees of Western Reserve University who delegated to President Thwing the task of securing the necessary funds. That task he accomplished with distinction.

C. C. Williamson at Western Reserve University

The accidental presence of C. C. Williamson on the Western Reserve campus at the time the endowment was made and his knowledge of the Carnegie grant through his serving as secretary to President Thwing add an unexpected relevance to his selection by the Carnegie Corporation to undertake the study on library training in 1919. Equally coincidental is the fact that two concepts later regarded by Williamson as fundamental to the improvement of library training: (1) that a library school be associated with a university; (2) that a college degree be an admission requirement, were concepts of the committee seeking the establishment of the Western Reserve University Library School.

Williamson gives the following account of the events leading to the establishment of the Library School, about which he knew because of his position as secretary to President Thwing from 1900 to 1905:

> I do not know now [i. e. in June, 1955], perhaps never did know, whose idea it was in the beginning to approach Mr. Carnegie for funds to start a library school in Cleveland. I think most likely it was Mr. William H. Brett's idea, but the stimulus might have originated with President Thwing himself, or with Linda Eastman, Ed Williams, or Electra VanDoren [i. e. Electra C. Doren], of Dayton. Williams was the only library school graduate in the group.

It was probably in the winter or early spring of 1904 [should be 1903?] that President Thwing arranged for an appointment and went to New York to see Mr. Carnegie. He returned with only a promise that the request would be considered. Some weeks elapsed with no word from New York. Then while President Thwing was absent for several days a letter arrived from Andrew Carnegie--a letter I opened with pent-up excitement. In it were bonds of the American Tobacco Company in an amount sufficient to yield an annual income of some $5,000. (I rely solely on memory for these details.) Dr. Thwing had instructed me to be on the lookout for the letter but not to tell anyone what it contained, or even of the receipt of a letter, until his return. I kept the secret, but it was a pretty tough job![27]

To the Carnegie Library of Pittsburgh, 1903

Less spectacular but equally eventful was the offer made in 1903 by Andrew Carnegie to the Board of Trustees of the Carnegie Library of Pittsburgh that he be permitted to contribute $5,000 for the ensuing three years toward the maintenance of the Carnegie Library Training School for Children's Librarians.[28]

The Training School for Children's Librarians had been in existence since September, 1901, when it had been organized, with a class of thirteen, because of the expanding interest in children's work and the creation of a separate children's department in April, 1898. The Training School was an outgrowth of the first training class organized in October, 1900, with five students. In 1903, because of his interest in the work, Carnegie made a gift, less generous than that made to Western Reserve University, but to a program entirely different--a specialized training program already operative in a public library.

The financial aid was continued until 1916, at which

time the School became a department of the Carnegie Institute, an institution endowed by Andrew Carnegie. In that year the name of the School was changed officially to the Carnegie Library School and it continued to receive a yearly budgetary allotment from the Institute.[29] Despite the emergence of a new financial pattern, the School continued, however, to be under the directorship of the librarian of the Carnegie Library of Pittsburgh. The complex financial and administrative pattern of the School continued until its official demise in 1962.

To the Carnegie Library of Atlanta, 1905

Andrew Carnegie's third grant was to the Carnegie Library of Atlanta which acknowledged that it could not continue to serve as an unofficial training center for its neighboring libraries. Concerned over the continuing loss of staff, Anne Wallace, librarian, appealed personally to Andrew Carnegie and he responded by making a gift of $4,000 yearly for three years, for the purpose of establishing a training program. He intimated further that if the School were successful, he would continue to make an annual grant.[30] The announcement of the gift was made on April 13, 1905.

Unlike the School established at Western Reserve University, the Atlanta School, first called the Southern Library School,[31] required only a high school degree or its equivalent and the passing of an entrance examination for admission to its one-year program. Julia Rankin, a graduate of the Pratt Institute Library School, was appointed instructor though the School itself was under the general direction of Miss Wallace.

Background of the Inquiry   11

To the New York Public Library, 1911

Not only did Andrew Carnegie contribute the funds for the building of the New York Public Library, he was persuaded to make five yearly appropriations of $15,000 for the establishment of a library school within the library. It was to be for a two-fold purpose: "to provide the New York Public Library and its branches with trained assistants and to fit for library positions elsewhere suitable candidates who do not wish to remain in New York."[32]

The first information pertaining to the School simply stated that "the Directors of the New York Public Library have announced the proposed establishment of a library school."[33] The directors referred to were John S. Billings, who had been president of the American Library Association in 1902 when Andrew Carnegie had donated funds to the Association,[34] and Edwin Hatfield Anderson. The latter, because of his experience with the library training programs at the Carnegie Library of Pittsburgh and later as director of the New York State Library School, was able both to offer practical suggestions and to teach the courses in administration in the School.[35]

The School was successful in securing as principal, Mary Wright Plummer,[36] director of the Pratt Institute Library School, whose lengthy experience had equipped her to organize the School. On a two-year plan, it offered in the first year a course of study similar to that in most of the one-year library schools and, in the second, a year of paid practice interspersed with lectures. The second-year program soon was changed to one which included subjects and books for discussion, for which there was not time in the first year. It also encouraged the pursuit of social studies at the New York School of Social Work.

At the end of the five-year period during which the School had received its promised support, the Carnegie Corporation continued to make annual appropriations, but in 1918 it appended to the appropriation bill the following resolution:

> The Board of Trustees of this Corporation has in view an inquiry into the subject of schools for training, the result of which may change its attitude in a particular case. [37]

The cryptic intent and the resultant actions of the resolution will be examined in detail in the chapters pertaining to the Williamson report on <u>Training for Library Work</u> of 1921.

Williamson's associations with the New York Public Library School

Because of C. C. Williamson's appointment to direct the study for the Carnegie Corporation, it seems pertinent to record his associations with another of the four schools which had received Carnegie grants. Williamson, appointed head of the Economics Division of the New York Public Library soon after its opening, was invited by Miss Plummer, principal of the School, to be one of the lecturers in the School. Miss Plummer, in her report which appeared in January, 1912, stated that

> A course likely to be developed into a larger one next year was that of three lectures by Dr. C. C. Williamson, lately of Bryn Mawr College, and now head of the economics division of the New York Public Library, on the literature of economics, of sociology, and of political science. [38]

Several references appear in ensuing reports indicating that Williamson continued his association with the School, lecturing, for example, on "Municipal library reference work" in 1915. [39]

As a lecturer his association with the School was min-

Background of the Inquiry   13

imal, but his experience did qualify him to make some
comments on the New York Public Library School in the
report which he was later to present to the Carnegie Corporation in 1921.

Summary

The four training programs referred to in this
chapter composed the "Carnegie Schools" only because of
the common source of their endowments or appropriations.
This factor in no way unified the schools. When the Williamson report was being prepared, however, Williamson was
obligated to view the schools more critically than the other
schools which had been established without benefit of Carnegie
money. In the accompanying chapter when the schools are
referred to there will be no attempt to group them as a
unit. They were, from the time of their establishment,
viewed by the Committee on Library Training[40] on individual
merit; therefore, references, when made, will be made on
that basis.

Three Factors Which Led to the Corporation's Inquiry

When, on March 11, 1918, the Carnegie Corporation
appended a resolution to the appropriation for the New York
Public Library School that it had "in view an inquiry into
the subject of schools for training librarians, the result of
which may change its attitude in a particular case," James
Bertram, secretary of the Corporation, prepared for the
Trustees a confidential memorandum[41] in which he so
persuasively outlined the need of a study that at the meeting
of March 28, 1919, the Trustees formally authorized the
undertaking of the Study of Training for Library Work and
approved the appointment of C. C. Williamson as director of

the Study. Before examining Williamson's study it seems appropriate to examine some of the factors which led to the Corporation's inquiry into the subject. Three of the factors may be identified as: (1) the need of a policy in regard to aiding library schools; (2) concern over the problems of the small Carnegie libraries which resulted in the Corporation's sponsoring a study by Alvin S. Johnson on "The Policy of Donations to Free Public Libraries"; (3) the attitude of James Bertram, secretary of the Corporation, toward libraries, librarians, and library training. Each of the three factors will be discussed.

The Need of a Policy in Regard to Aiding Library Schools

The resolution implied that the Corporation had not formulated an official policy in regard to library training. Though the attitude of the Corporation had been, since its incorporation in 1911, that of Andrew Carnegie, it was well known that despite the philosophy Carnegie had endowed or was supporting four library schools. The reference to "a particular case" could have been directed either (1) to the schools at that time receiving appropriations; or (2) to institutions seeking aid in establishing new schools.

To the Schools Receiving Appropriations

Two schools were receiving direct appropriations in 1918: the Library School of the Carnegie Library of Atlanta and the New York Public Library School. Neither the Carnegie Library School of Pittsburgh nor the Library School of Western Reserve, however, was receiving direct appropriations. The Carnegie Library School, which from 1903 to 1916 had received some support from Andrew Carnegie, was being supported by funds from the Carnegie Institute

Background of the Inquiry   15

which Andrew Carnegie had established and endowed for educational purposes. The Library School of Western Reserve had received no additional support since its endowment in 1903.

Whatever the intention of the study, it is evident that the four schools named would receive special attention in a report to be made to the Corporation.

To Institutions Seeking Appropriations
for Aid in Establishing New Schools

The particular attention given to the following schools or institutions in the report to the Corporation in 1921, entitled "Training for Library Work," indicates that they were probably seeking aid from the Corporation. They were: (1) the Portland, Oregon, Public Library; (2) the Riverside (California) Library Service School; (3) Simmons College.

Of the Portland situation, Williamson wrote:

> When this study was first proposed, my attention was called to the fact that the Portland (Oregon) Public Library, officially known as the Library Association of Portland, had for some time been hoping to start a library school. . . . Miss Frances Isom . . . was untiring in her efforts to interest the Carnegie Corporation in her project.[42]

Of the Riverside Library Service School Williamson acknowledged that

> Though I have not been informed that the Riverside Library Service School was seeking endowment from the Carnegie Corporation, I inferred that such was the case.[43]

Williamson apparently had not been fully informed of the efforts being exerted on behalf of Simmons College either, for he noted

> As this report was nearing completion it was learned that some special reference to the Simmons

College School of Library Science might be in order.[44]

Though efforts of the University of California to secure an endowment were not cited, Joseph Cummings Rowell, librarian of the University, as early as 1903, had urged President Wheeler to write to Andrew Carnegie concerning the establishment of a library school in California.[45] Despite the timeliness of his request, following so soon after the endowment made to Western Reserve University, Wheeler acknowledged in October of 1903 that he had received no response from Andrew Carnegie.[46] The recommendation, made by Williamson eighteen years later, that a school at the University be partially subsidized by the Corporation was a belated fulfillment of Rowell's initial request. There is no evidence within the report, however, that Rowell's efforts prompted Williamson's examination of the situation at the University of California.

Concern Over the Problems of the Small Carnegie Libraries

The proliferation of Carnegie library buildings throughout the country led eventually to the serious problem of ineffectual services, for though provisions were made for the building of sturdy monuments, little attention was given to the function and contents of the buildings. Nor did the situation seem remediable, for according to the "Letter of Promise" exchanged between Andrew Carnegie and a community, the recipient of a library building, only two conditions were to be met:

> First, that the community should provide the site, and second, that the City Council appropriate by taxation not less than ten per cent of of the cost of the building for maintenance.[47]

For example, of 1317 libraries built, 1048, or 80 per cent, cost less than $10,000. Should the communities owning those

Background of the Inquiry   17

libraries have fulfilled even the minimal requirement of the "Letter of Promise," the annual budget for those libraries would have been about $1,000, from which the librarian's salary, library materials, and maintenance charges would have been taken. [48]

By 1915 the League of Library Commissions was writing to the Carnegie Corporation that the ten per cent clause had frequently been detrimental in communities which felt that by meeting that minimum their obligations had been fulfilled. The League attempted

> to ascertain whether in case you regard it merely as a minimum your office would be willing to make a clearer or more definite statement to that effect. [49]

James Bertram, secretary of the Corporation, in reply, acknowledged the difficulty of estimating accurately the amount needed but added that

> ten per cent of the cost of bilding for maintenance seems a fair average for the country as a whole, and of course we could not discriminate between sections. [50]

He did, however, point out that "our letter of promis wil show that we leav this matter of the amount of the pledge elastic, with 10% as the minimum."

The Corporation evidenced more concern than Bertram's letter implied, for at the meeting of the Board of Trustees on November 18, 1915, the Executive Committee was authorized

> to employ a man of high qualifications to examine and report to the Corporation upon the results of the wide provision of Public Library Buildings by Mr. Carnegie and this Corporation, with such recommendations as his study may lead him to propose. [51]

The "man of high qualifications" selected was Alvin Saunders Johnson,[52] who, according to Robert M. Lester, secretary

of the Carnegie Corporation from 1934 to 1954, not only was
asked to study the results of wide provision of free public
library buildings but also to inquire into library schools and
the adequacy of the output of trained librarians. [53]

Though Johnson submitted his Report in 1916, its
recommendation that the Carnegie Corporation continue its
policy of donations guided by certain principles of "philanthropic intervention"[54] advanced in the Report, was rejected
by the Corporation, for in 1917 the Corporation discontinued
its practice of making grants for the erection of library
buildings. [55] The Report was not totally ineffectual, however,
for Johnson directed his attention not only to policies of
donations for library buildings, but proposed a program
wherein the Corporation would shift its emphasis to library
service and to the promotion of a broader concept of library
training. It is with that second aspect of the Johnson Report
that this study is concerned.

The Johnson Report on the Policy of Donations
to Free Public Libraries

Robert Lester's definition of the scope of the study
to be undertaken by Alvin S. Johnson more nearly defines
the scope than does the original resolution authorizing it,
for Johnson acknowledged that his suggestions had gone far
beyond the work of library establishment to that of library
service. He justified broadening the scope by emphasizing
that

> It is the library as a going concern, not the
> library as a piece of architecture, that the
> Carnegie Corporation has sought to promote. In
> the present state of library development, the
> library as a going concern . . . will best be
> promoted by a policy that includes particular
> attention to conditions of service. [56]

Background of the Inquiry

In viewing the conditions of service, Johnson encountered the problems resulting not only from the small libraries' attempts to fulfill the terms of the "letter of promise" but, even more, from deliquencies among libraries not fulfilling the promise. He, as Bertram had done earlier, agreed that it would be psychologically unwise to change the existing percentage basis despite the obvious inadequacy of ten per cent but added that a community should be fully informed "as to the meaning of effective library work and the probable cost of it."[57]

From his survey of library personnel only a dismal picture emerged. Johnson cited particularly the fact that in many instances training had been regarded as secondary to other qualifications such as "local, social and political standing"[58] and observed that "if the chief librarian is of indifferent quality--not an uncommon case--the home-bred stuff reflects all her weaknesses."[59]

While recognizing that the Corporation could not attempt to seek as a prerequisite the services of properly qualified personnel, Johnson emphasized the importance of discussing the subject, claiming that

> an inactive library is not only a questionable investment of capital, but it operates to propagate erroneous notions as to the futility of public sacrifices for library purposes.[60]

Having characterized an "inactive library," he asserted that "nothing makes more certainly for library inactivity than an untrained and unintelligent librarian."[61]

Some observations on library training. --Johnson's own convictions concerning the limitations of the "untrained and unintelligent librarian" were strengthened by his own survey of facilities for library training. Johnson unhesitatingly stated that of the thirteen institutions offering professional

training, only seven were of much importance. Those he
identified as being three in New York, one in Massachusetts,
one in Pennsylvania; one in Wisconsin, and one in Illinois.
The schools may easily be enumerated as the New York
State Library School, the Pratt Institute Library School, the
New York Public Library School, Simmons College Library
School, the Carnegie Library School (Pittsburgh), University
of Wisconsin Library School, and the University of Illinois
Library School. Omitted from the list were the names of
two schools: Western Reserve University Library School,
which had received a Carnegie endowment, and the Library
School of the Carnegie Library of Atlanta which was, at the
time of Johnson's Report, receiving an annual subsidy.

Two weaknesses in the training programs cited by
Johnson were: (1) the expenditure of time on technical
subjects at the expense of emphasizing the reading interests
of a community; (2) the adaptation of the training to the
needs of large libraries rather than to the work of the
smaller libraries of the Carnegie type. Johnson deplored
the emphasis on technical training, not in itself, but in that
it was, according to many entrance requirements, super-
imposed upon a high school education. He concluded:

> Now, it appears self-evident that one year of
> technical training, superimposed upon a high
> school education, is not sufficient to place a
> librarian in a position to assert for the library
> its proper place in the community. 62

He expressed skepticism also concerning the combination of
a college course with one year of professional training.

Johnson did not advocate, as did C. C. Williamson
later, that the minimal entrance requirement to library
schools be a college degree, though he had freely expressed
doubts about admission to high school graduates and even

Background of the Inquiry   21

about the combination four-year program. Within the confines of his assignment, to make recommendations to the Carnegie Corporation, he proposed that the Corporation, working through state library commissions, foster the establishment "in a number of state universities of combined academic and professional library courses."[63]

Anticipating the objection that it seemed questionable to provide additional facilities for library training as long as librarians remained underpaid, Johnson admitted that in view of the passivity and inefficiency of library personnel the profession was receiving quite all that it deserved.[64] His own proposal for providing additional facilities was predicated on the assumption that "improvement of service must, as a rule, be prior to increased remuneration at the hands of public authorities," and that to encourage improvement of service, the Corporation might well consider the problems of training.

Convinced that the Corporation "might properly take measures to increase the number of persons trained for library work," he offered four recommendations in addition to the one pertaining to the fostering of combined academic and professional library courses. They were: (1) to create scholarships
> in established library schools open to persons possessing the requisite educational diploma--who have served not less than one year in practical library work;[65]

(2) to subsidize summer library courses in universities for librarians of small libraries; (3) to assist existing library schools to increase their facilities or encourage certain institutions to undertake library instruction; (4) to exert influence on training, shifting the emphasis from buildings to service.[66]

Through these recommendations the Carnegie Corporation was advised in 1916 to broaden its concept of responsibility of library training for improved library service. It was not, however, until March 11, 1918, that the Corporation announced its intention of inquiring into the subject of library training. Even though no reference to the Johnson Report appeared in the resolution pertaining to the proposed inquiry, it would appear that Johnson's analysis of the relation of ineffectual service to the training of the librarian was ultimately more effectual than his recommendations concerning the policy of donating library buildings.

James Bertram's Reference to the Johnson Report

Bertram referred briefly to the Johnson Report in the Memorandum which he prepared for the Trustees "with the view of giving them some idea of the problems of library schools."[67] He did not, however, include Johnson's recommendations or discussion on library training; rather, he cited Johnson's reference to the inefficient and ineffectual service being offered by libraries. The Memorandum reads:

> As Dr. Johnson says in his report, one reason for libraries not giving the service which might be expected of them is the lack of a continuing accession of books and a consequent falling away of interest, resulting in an attitude of neglect on the part of the community toward the pledge of tax revenue given by their selected representatives in order to secure the library building.[68]

Bertram's deliberate omission from the Memorandum of Johnson's analysis of the facilities for library training might imply that the Report was less than satisfactory to the Corporation; his failure to include any critical comments on Johnson's recommendations indicates that by 1918 the Report was being neglected.

Background of the Inquiry   23

C. C. Williamson's Reference to the Johnson Report

    Williamson did not refer to Johnson or to the Report in the first contribution which he made following his discussions with Bertram concerning the problems of libraries and training. Nevertheless, his article, "The Need of a Plan for Library Development,"[69] appears in a sense to be a rebuttal of Johnson's ideas and much more condemnatory of the small town librarian, of the American Library Association, and of library schools.

    Williamson did make a brief evaluative comment on Johnson later when he prepared his confidential memorandum on "Notes on the Aims, Scope and Method of the Study of Training for Library Service . . . to be held Wednesday, April 28, 1920."[70] Though admitting that the Johnson Report had "brought the matter specifically before the Corporation,"[71] Williamson criticized the report as containing "nothing particularly new to the library profession" and concluded:

> Many of his observations as to conditions and needs are pertinent and valuable, but his suggestions as to methods for the improvement and extension of training facilities were either very general or of questionable practicability.[72]

Similarities of the Johnson and Williamson reports. -- Despite Williamson's deprecations of Johnson's Report, the two reports were strikingly similar in their suggestions for the improvement of training. Both urged that a prerequisite for admission to library schools be a college degree, though, to be sure, it was Williamson who definitely stated that prerequisite as being one of the fundamental concepts of his study. Both advised the Corporation to assist existing schools to increase their facilities; both advocated a changing of emphasis in the content of the curriculum; both recommended that a program of scholarships be instituted. Though Johnson had spoken favorably of the American Library Association,[73] and had proposed certain activities which it could undertake if it were subsidized, Williamson was less impressed with it. Yet he too urged that the Corporation give aid whenever a concrete proposal endorsed by the profession emerged. In his only reference to the Association in his final summary prepared for the Board of Trustees, Williamson acknowledged that "it is conceivable that the Corporation might work through the American Library Association."[74] The implementation of Williamson's recommendations may, in some instances, be regarded as delayed action on the Johnson Report, presented in 1916.

James Bertram's Attitude

After the establishment of the Carnegie Corporation of New York in 1911, the Corporation was directed by an Executive Committee of three: Andrew Carnegie, president; James Bertram, secretary; and Robert A. Franks, treasurer.[75] Of the three, Bertram, acting as Corporation secretary and as confidential secretary to Carnegie, bore the major responsibility for furthering the aims of the Corporation, aims identified in Bertram's mind as those of Carnegie.

Despite Carnegie's interest in libraries, Bertram's own relation to libraries and librarians in the early years of the Corporation were less than cordial. He knew few librarians or secretaries of state library commissions personally. He did not attend library conferences, where he could have gained some understanding of the problems and of the concern with the education of librarians.

According to Frank P. Hill, Bertram depended on the

Background of the Inquiry   25

counsel of a few librarians, two of them being William H.
Brett, who had successfully secured a Carnegie grant for
the establishment of a library school at Western Reserve
University, and Henry N. Sanborn, at one time secretary
of the Indiana Library Commission and later librarian of
Bridgeport, Connecticut, Public Libraries.[76] Bertram's
lack of familiarity with the profession presumably accounted
in part for the indictment made by him in the Memorandum,
in which he concluded:

> It would seem that, considering the admitted
> inadequacy of library training facilities, one
> might fairly expect enough initiative and force
> to manifest itself in one or all of these bodies
> at least to cause the situation to be canvassed,
> and make known what is necessary to be done.
> However, although it seems surprising that these
> bodies should year after year meet to discuss
> library matters and never effectually deal with
> the problem of the inadequacy of library training
> facilities, such is the case.[77]

There is no evidence that Bertram either had made
a study of the reports of the Committee on Library Training
or that he had consulted the Association of American Library
Schools before making the indictment. Had he consulted the
Committee or the Association neither could have repudiated
the charge of inadequacy, but the omission of their efforts
from the Memorandum reflects either the unfamiliarity of
the writer with his topic or a determined effort to ignore
them.

Even while charging the Association with failure to
deal effectively with the problem of the inadequacy of library
training facilities, Bertram's own opinion that unschooled
librarians would be employed in small libraries because of
low salaries was apparently well known. The Library Journal
included a reference to his opinion in September, 1918, which

read:

> It has been frequently emphasized, not least by Mr. James Bertram from the experience of the Carnegie Corporation, that unschooled librarians are and must always be in demand for the thousands of little libraries which cannot afford to pay salaries for full trained service. Dr. Williamson, in his paper in this issue, further explains this thought and makes some suggestions of interest for the education of the unprofessional librarian. 78

While similarities between Bertram's ideas and those contained in Williamson's "The Need of a Plan for Library Development"79 could have been accidental, the content reflected accurate editorializing. Bertram later stated in the Memorandum that the paper had been prepared after several conferences between himself and Williamson and that it included

> most of the points upon which he and the writer found themselves agreed (which could be stated to librarians by Mr. Williamson, and not by an outsider). 80

Though Williamson's paper made no reference to Bertram or to the Corporation, its importance in substantiating Bertram's opinions, its inclusion in the Memorandum, and its possible influence on the decision by the Trustees to undertake a study of library training add unusual significance to the content of Williamson's analysis of the need of a plan for library development.

Because of its importance in reflecting the attitude of both Williamson and Bertram on training for library work as well as library work itself, and more specifically, the training of the unprofessional librarian serving in small libraries bearing the name "Carnegie," the contents will be examined in the accompanying section.

Background of the Inquiry 27

The Need of a Plan for Library Development

"The Need of a Plan,"[81] when read in the knowledge that it was expressing the views of Bertram, and through him the Corporation's, was in essence a warning to the library profession that it was failing in its provision of service, particularly in the small Carnegie libraries, and likewise in its provision of training for librarians of small libraries. The article further warned that the responsibility for improvement or advances rested squarely upon the profession and was not the responsibility of an outside institution. Indeed such a warning was stated thus:

> Public authorities and private philanthropists will not hesitate to invest in the execution of plans which will insure large returns in public service for a given expenditure of money. But neither public officials nor philanthropists will venture to furnish both the plans and the money and then thrust their work upon a hostile or even upon an indifferent profession.[82]

<u>Williamson's view of library service and librarians.</u> -- Williamson sketched a bleak picture of the small library in which the librarian was "unconscious of any shortcomings in the service, or in her own equipment and capacity," and of the library boards, some of whom "were even more visionless and ineffective than the librarian herself." Williamson reprimanded librarians for regarding the situation as hopeless until the communities could provide the salary of a fully trained professional librarian and stated that such an attitude "is at bottom one of impotence, helplessness, indifference."[83] Stressing that ineffectual library service was due largely to ineffectual librarians, and that the public should not be blamed for its disinterest in an inactive and stagnant library, he observed:

> A person with moderate training and some in-

genuity can produce valuable results with meagre support, but an untrained and sluggish librarian will do nothing worth while no matter how generous the support. [84]

Williamson did, however, recognize the economic issue, for he asked, "May not the real problem be that the best talent in the library profession has been seeking professional distinction in more lucrative fields?"[85] Having thus implied that the best talent avoided service in small libraries, Williamson suggested, not that higher salaries be offered for better trained people, but rather that the American Library Association "work out some plan of professional education that would be adequate for the needs of every branch of library service."[86]

Williamson on library training. -- Williamson examined the agencies of training, noting the services of the state library commissions, summer schools, library institutes.[87] Of the existing library schools, Williamson observed that: (1) they were "not attempting to fit students for part time positions paying $30 to $50 a month";[88] (2) library school facilities were inadequate to meet the need for trained personnel in the higher ranks; (3) existing schools were doing good work though perhaps the courses were not flexible enough for the great diversity of requirements in the positions which the graduates accepted; (4) the capacity of the schools was not equal to the demand.

The accuracy of the first statement could not, and would not have been disputed by the library schools. Its fairness, however, could have been challenged on many points, one being that of realistic economy. Unless persons receiving such minimal salaries were financially independent, they could not have pursued library training in the regular schools, knowing that their income would be from $30 to $50.

Background of the Inquiry   29

Further, a part-time library position was--and is--part-time because of limited local funds, need, and staff, not because the work required half-doing.

Statements two and three are somewhat supplementary in the observations that library schools were inadequate yet were doing "good work" for certain levels of positions. The dubious equation of capacity with demand in statement four was countered by the admission from Williamson that the library schools were having "difficulty in recruiting students up to their full capacity," but he stated that he regarded a continuing shortage of students as another incentive for self-examination and planning for the future.

Williamson's suggestions for improving the situation. -- Of the three suggestions in regard to library training, not one was a totally new idea. In not one, however, did Williamson acknowledge that the profession had given some consideration to each idea. His suggestions pertained to (1) a graduate school; (2) correspondence courses; (3) the establishment of an agency to coordinate the varied training programs in existence.

Concerning a graduate school. -- Melvil Dewey, as early as 1888, had proposed a post-graduate course. Some years later, in 1900, Aksel G. S. Josephson advocated in his "Preparation for Librarianship" the organization of an "independent post-graduate university course, in connection with some university, with a large staff of instructors and rich libraries." Then in 1917, only fifteen months before Williamson's article appeared, Josephson urged again "the absolute necessity of the establishment by some university of a course in bibliography and library administration for library school graduates and for graduate students in general."[89]

Yet Williamson made no reference to the earlier proposals; he simply offered the following thought:

> I have wondered whether it would be possible or desirable to establish a purely graduate school of very high order, to which only graduates of other schools or those with equivalent training and some successful experience would be admitted. This would enable existing schools and the others we shall need to confine their energies to the fundamental things that every grade of service requires. A graduate school, especially if conducted as a part of a university, could afford more specialized work than can be expected of any existing school. 90

Concerning correspondence courses. -- Having viewed the various types of training available to the librarian of the small library, Williamson proposed another: the adaptation of the correspondence method of instruction. Williamson warned, however,

> I do not propose this as a substitute for anything else, but merely as the necessary and logical supplement to other methods -- the lowest round of the ladder, if you please, the step that it would be relatively easy to persuade every one to take and which would lead naturally and easily to other higher steps. 91

In recommending an adaptation of the correspondence method of instruction for the librarians of small libraries, Williamson was again repeating a proposal made by Melvil Dewey in 1888, but in this instance Williamson acknowledged that after having become interested in the idea of correspondence training for special library service, and later, for small library service, he had learned that

> Melvil Dewey, many years ago, believed a correspondence course feasible and wished the Albany school to become the pioneer in establishing one. 92

Williamson failed to make references to the reports of the

Background of the Inquiry   31

Committee on Library Training which would have given more
up-to-date information on correspondence work and would
have indicated further that library schools were not unaware of the training problem. The reports, while indicating a vacillating policy by the Committee, nevertheless
show that in 1903 the Committee had recommended that some
of the established schools and/or leading libraries be
authorized by the Association to offer correspondence work;
that the 1905 Standards of Library Training failed to define
standards for correspondence work; that in 1906 the Committee decided to suggest no standards or regulations for
correspondence courses; that in 1907 the Committee had,
despite its 1906 decision, commented unfavorably on the
program sponsored by the International Correspondence
University.

Because of Williamson's tentative proposal to make
use of the correspondence method of instruction, it is
interesting to note that he became increasingly convinced
of its merits and in his report to the Carnegie Corporation
made a specific recommendation that, should a library
school be established in New York City with Carnegie funds,
it "should be expected to develop this work [i.e. correspondence study] on a large scale, to put into it the best
available organizing and teaching ability."93

Concerning the establishment of an agency. -- In
viewing the diversity of the training agencies Williamson
recognized the need to coordinate the training programs
being offered or to be offered to the librarian of the small
library. He proposed, consequently, the creation of

> Some central organization, a library service
> bureau perhaps, under the management of a
> board chosen by the [state library] commissions
> and existing professional organizations, [which]

should work out plans and supervise their execution, assigning to each agency the tasks it is fitted to undertake. [94]

Within Williamson's proposal for a central organization, functioning as a coordinating body for various types of training, lies the germinal seed for his advocacy of an American Library Association Training Board about which he was to speak in 1919 at the Asbury Park Conference. In proposing the creation of a central organization, Williamson might well have related his concept of an organization to that premature plan proposed by William H. Brett in 1898,[95] for an examining board which would, in effect, have unified the various training agencies through its program of examination and awarding of degrees and diplomas. He did not, however, make any reference to Brett's plan which up to that time had failed to materialize.

Reception of Williamson's Study on "The Need of a Plan"

Williamson's exploration of the need of a plan brought forth in response only the brief editorial comment, previously cited, in Library Journal, which identified the thoughts as being similar to those of James Bertram. As a gentle rebuff the editorial called attention to the use of institutes in training programs, which Williamson had presumably overlooked. It offered, however, no defense for the ineptitude of the librarians as charged or for the programs of the library schools. Neither, moreover, did the American Library Association nor the library schools respond directly to the implications in the article; however, at the March 1919 meeting of the Association of American Library Schools, Sarah C. N. Bogle discussed formally Williamson's "The Need of a Plan for Library Development."[96]

Background of the Inquiry

Librarians, both in small and large libraries, might have been dismayed by the devastating presentation of the library situation. In summary the article observed that (1) ineffectual library service was due largely to ineffectual librarians; (2) the responsibility of finding practicable means for minimum training for librarians of small libraries was in itself a professional responsibility; (3) both librarians and training agencies had failed to accept the responsibility; (4) a possible solution to the problem lay in the creation of a central bureau designed to coordinate training for various levels of service.

In accepting Bertram's statement that the article expressed his sentiments, [97] one can only conclude that librarians, the library profession, and the American Library Association were held in low esteem by him. Also that such a conclusion seems justified is supported by an examination of the Memorandum prepared by Bertram for the Corporation during the year, 1918.

Notes

1. "Western Reserve University Library School," LJ, XXX (March, 1905), 165. Carnegie also added that of all the occupations, "I think I would be happiest if I had charge of a library."

2. Letter from Melvil Dewey, May 21, 1890, quoted in Grosvenor Dawe, Melvil Dewey, Seer, Inspirer, Doer, 1851-1931 (Essex Co., N.Y.: Lake Placid Club, 1932), p. 333.

3. Carnegie Corporation of New York, Memorandum Concerning Library Schools, 1918 (New York, 1918), p. 3. (in the files of the Corporation.) Cited hereafter as Carnegie Corporation of New York, Memorandum.

4. Ibid.

5. "Minutes of the Regents, July 10, 1899," quoted in New York State Library School, The First Quarter Century of the New York State Library School, 1887-1912 (New York: Education Department, New York State Library School, 1912), p. 22-23. Details relating to the transfer may be found in Ray Trautman, A History of the School of Library Service. Columbia University (New York: Columbia University Press, 1954).

6. Andrew Carnegie, "The Best Fields for Philanthropy," The North American Review, CLXIX (December, 1889), 688-690.

7. Letter from Melvil Dewey, May 12, 1890, quoted in Dawe, p. 201.

8. Letter from Andrew Carnegie, May 15, 1890, quoted in Dawe, p. 200.

9. Letter from Melvil Dewey, May 21, 1890, quoted in Dawe, p. 332-335.

10. Alvin S. Johnson, A Report to Carnegie Corporation of New York on the Policy of Donations to Free Public Libraries (n. p., n. d.), p. 65. Johnson suggested that "the Corporation might properly take measures to increase the number of persons trained for library work."

11. Charles Clarence Williamson, Andrew Carnegie: His Contribution to the Public Library Movement; a Commemorative Address. Founders' Day Address, Delivered at the Library School, Western Reserve University (Cleveland: Western Reserve University, 1920), p. 14. Williamson said, "I believe I but voice the feeling of all qualified observers in saying that he has done more to promote free libraries in the highest sense through these library schools than through any like expenditure of money for buildings."

12. Letter from Melvil Dewey, May 21, 1890, quoted in Dawe, p. 333.

13. Ibid., p. 334.

14. Ibid., p. 335.

15. Trautman, op. cit., p. 29.

16. Ibid., p. 33.

Background of the Inquiry

17. "Carnegie Endowment for Library Training School," LJ, XXVIII (March, 1903), 118.

18. ["The Carnegie Library School Endowment to Western Reserve" -- Editorial comment], LJ, XXVIII (March, 1903), 103.

19. ["Western Reserve; Extracts from the Cleveland Plain Dealer" - Editorial comment], PL, VIII (April, 1903), 152.

20. Ohio Library Association, "Proceedings of a Sixth Annual Meeting," PL, V (Nov., 1900), 358-360.

21. "Report on Library Training," PL, V (Dec., 1900), 426.

22. Ohio Library Association, "Proceedings of a Sixth Annual Meeting," p. 360.

23. Linda A. Eastman, Portrait of a Librarian (Chicago: American Library Association, 1940), p. 48.

24. Miss Eastman makes no reference to the committee in her biography of Brett, but states that: "He [Brett] evolved a plan for a library school, as a new department of the Western Reserve University; in which he believed that certain of the bibliographical and book courses could be given advantageously by the University professors, and the technical instruction by trained library school teachers and members of the library staff, while the public and university libraries would afford opportunity for practice work." Ibid.

25. The Committee members were all from Cleveland: Allen D. Severance, of the College for Women; W. H. Brett and Linda Eastman, of the Cleveland Public Library; E. C. Williams of the library of Western Reserve University.
   C. C. Williamson praised the work of E. C. Williams, a Negro, who had been graduated from Adelbert College at the head of his class in 1892. Two years after graduation he was appointed librarian of the College. He attended the Amherst Summer School of Library Economy in the summer of 1895 and later received an honor first-year certificate for the year, 1899-1900, spent at the New York State Library School. C. C. Williamson, Statement Prepared for the Use of Miss Sarah K. Vann, June, 1955, p. 5.

26. "For a Library School at Western Reserve University," LJ, XXVI (June, 1901), 336.

27. Williamson, Statement. June, 1955, p. 7-8.

28. "Carnegie Library Training School for Children's Librarians," LJ, XXXVIII (May, 1908), 252.

29. Elva S. Smith, "The Carnegie Library School--a Bit of History," LJ, XLVI (Oct. 1, 1921), 791-794.

30. "Atlanta, Ga. Carnegie L[ibrary]," LJ, XXX (April, 1905), 236.

31. "Southern Library School: Carnegie Library of Atlanta," LJ, XXX (June, 1905), 363. The name was changed in 1907 to the Library Training School of the Carnegie Library of Atlanta. "Southern Library School," LJ, XXXII (Aug., 1907), 375. Additional information on the School may be found in Anne Wallace Howland, "The Library Movement in the South Since 1899," LJ, XXXII (June, 1907), 253-258.

32. "New York Public Library School," LJ, XXXVI (June, 1911), 303.

33. Ibid.

34. Carnegie's first contribution for the improvement of services in the library buildings which he had donated was a "donation for the preparation and publication of reading lists, indexes, and other bibliographical and literary aids." The announcement of the gift was made by John S. Billings, president of the American Library Association, in his presidential address on "Some Library Problems of To-morrow." John S. Billings, "Some Library Problems of To-morrow; Address of the President," LJ, XXVII (July, 1902), 9.

35. "New York Public Library School," LJ, XXXVI (July, 1911), 376.

36. Ibid.

37. Carnegie Corporation of New York, Memorandum, p. 3.

38. "New York Public Library - Library School," LJ, XXXVII (Jan., 1912), 37.

39. "Library School of the New York Public Library," LJ, XL (April, 1915), 276.

Background of the Inquiry   37

40.   The reports of the Committee on Library Training
are to be found in the Conference numbers of Library
Journal from 1900 to 1906, and in the Bulletin of the American Library Association from 1907 to 1924.

41.   Carnegie Corporation of New York, Memorandum.

42.   Williamson I, p. 196.

43.   Ibid., p. 207.

44.   Ibid., p. 288.

45.   Letter from Joseph Cummings Rowell, April 16,
1903. (in the archives of the University of California,
Berkeley). In the letter, addressed to President Benjamin
Ide Wheeler, Rowell outlined in detail the amount of money
needed for the School and referred to Carnegie's endowment
to Western Reserve University as offering "sufficient encouragement to suggest to Mr. Carnegie that this University
would undertake the work in the far west with the same
endowment. " ($100,000 yielding $6,000 annually).

46.   Letter from Benjamin Ide Wheeler, October 10, 1903.
(in the archives of the University of California, Berkeley).

47.   Frank Pierce Hill, James Bertram: an Appreciation
(New York: Carnegie Corporation of New York, 1936), p.
49.

48.   Carnegie Corporation of New York, Memorandum,
p. 4.

49.   Letter from J. I. Wyer, Jr., October 28, 1915,
quoted in Hill, p. 50.

50.   Letter from Jas. Bertram, November 1, 1915,
quoted in Hill, p. 51.

51.   Alvin S. Johnson, A Report to Carnegie Corporation
of New York on the Policy of Donations to Free Public
Libraries. (n.p., n.d.), p. 3.

52.   When asked to undertake the study for the Corporation,
Alvin Saunders Johnson was at Cornell University and was
serving also as editor of the New Republic. He later became associated with the New School of Social Research and

was an associate editor of the Encyclopaedia of the Social Sciences.

53. New Frontiers in Librarianship; Proceedings of the Special Meeting of the Association of American Library Schools and the Board of Education for Librarianship of the American Library Association in Honor of the University of Chicago and Graduate Library School, December 30, 1940 (Chicago: The University of Chicago, Graduate Library School, 1941), p. 5.

54. Johnson, op. cit., pp. 16, 17, 30, 31, 38, 42, 55.

55. At the meeting of the Board of Trustees on November 7, 1917, "it was decided that a sufficient demonstration had been made of the usefulness and need for public libraries and it was voted that no new application for the erection of library buildings be considered." Hill, op. cit., p. 35.

56. Johnson, op. cit., p. 68.

57. Ibid., p. 55.

58. Ibid., p. 40.

59. Ibid., p. 41.

60. Ibid., p. 43.

61. Ibid.

62. Johnson, op. cit., p. 47.

63. Ibid., p. 49. Williamson expressed disapproval of the combined academic and professional courses though at the time of his report he stated that more than fifty per cent of library school graduates had only three years of college to which had been added the fourth year in a library school. Williamson I, p. 96; Williamson II, p. 69.

64. Johnson, op. cit., p. 47.

65. Ibid., p. 65.

66. Ibid., p. 66.

67. Carnegie Corporation of New York, Memorandum, p. 6.

68.   Ibid., p. 4.

69.   C. C. Williamson, "The Need of a Plan for Library Development," LJ, XLIII (September, 1918), 649-654.

70.   C. C. Williamson, "Notes on the Aims, Scope and Method of the Study of Training for Library Service, for Discussion at the Meeting of the Advisory Committee, to be held Wednesday, April 28, 1920." (Typewritten copy, marked "Confidential," from the files of Williamson used for this study.)

71.   Ibid., p. 2.

72.   Ibid.

73.   Johnson had written, "There is reason for believing that the Association, if better provided with funds, could offer a richer and more practical service to the associated librarians." Johnson, op. cit., p. 67.

74.   C. C. Williamson, "Summary of Report on Training for Library Work, prepared for the Carnegie Corporation of New York," p. 16.

75.   Hill, op. cit., p. 34.

76.   Ibid., p. 43. In 1904 James Bertram had been serving as secretary since December 1, 1897, and it is possible that he had met W. H. Brett when the endowment to Western Reserve was being considered. Both the names of Brett and Sanborn appear on the list of persons recommended as possible committee members for the inquiry into library schools, prepared by Williamson on July 6, 1918.

77.   Carnegie Corporation of New York, Memorandum, p. 3.

78.   [Williamson's "The Need of a Plan for Library Development" -- Editorial comment], LJ. XLIII (September, 1918), 642.

79.   Williamson, "The Need of a Plan," pp. 649-655.

80.   Carnegie Corporation of New York, Memorandum, p. 6.

81. The article appeared first in the September, 1918, issue of Library Journal, two months after the Saratoga Conference of the American Library Association. At that Conference, Williamson, at the request of Bertram, had conferred with representative librarians concerning a proposed study of library training.
Though Bertram states in the Memorandum (p. 6) that the paper had been prepared for reading at the meeting of the American Library Association in July, 1918, there is no indication in the official proceedings of the Saratoga Conference that the paper was read.

82. Williamson, "The Need of a Plan," p. 650.

83. Ibid., p. 649.

84. Ibid., p. 651.

85. Ibid., p. 649.

86. Ibid.

87. Williamson's reference to library institutes gave no hint that they had been tried for years, the first record being of that held in Indianapolis, December 29-31, 1896, under the auspices of the Indiana Library Association. Other states which conducted institutes were Wisconsin, Massachusetts, Michigan, Pennsylvania, and New York. Nina K. Preston, "Library Institutes," PL, IX (December, 1904), 486-489.

88. Williamson, "The Need of a Plan," p. 652.

89. For a discussion of Josephson's plans see: Aksel G. S. Josephson, "Preparation for Librarianship," LJ, XXV (May, 1900), 226-28. Aksel G. S. Josephson, "Training for Librarianship," PL, XXII (June, 1917), 223-24. Josephson's concern had been expressed as early as 1896 in his "Is Librarianship a Learned Profession?" PL I (September, 1896), 195-96.

90. Williamson, "The Need of a Plan," p. 654. Within this concept of "a purely graduate school" lies the origin of Williamson's plan for advanced and specialized study, more clearly defined in his formal Corporation report.

91. Ibid., p. 652.

92. Ibid.

93. Williamson I, p. 193.

94. Ibid., p. 653.

95. American Library Association, "Proceedings, 1898," LJ, XXIII (August 1898), 124; 136.

96. Sarah C. N. Bogle, Discussion at the Annual Meeting of the Association of American Library Schools, Atlantic City, March 8, 1919, [on] "Need of a Plan for Library Development." (in the files of the Association).

97. On December 30, 1940, at the Graduate Library School of the University of Chicago, Robert M. Lester, secretary of the Carnegie Corporation, made a public reference to "The Need of a Plan," indicating that Bertram had asked Williamson to prepare a statement on library training facilities. At the time of its publication, however, few, if any, knew that the Carnegie Corporation had manifested an interest in the subject through Williamson. New Frontiers in Librarianship; Proceedings of the Special Meeting of the Association of American Library Schools and the Board of Education for Librarianship of the American Library Association, in honor of the University of Chicago and the Graduate Library School (Chicago: The Graduate Library School, University of Chicago, 1941).

Chapter 2

Bertram's Memorandum and Further Plans for the Study on Training

Memorandum Concerning Library Schools, 1918

After the Board of Trustees of the Carnegie Corporation had stated, on March 11, 1918, that it had "in view an inquiry into the subject of schools for training librarians," James Bertram prepared for the Trustees[1] a confidential Memorandum "with the view of giving them some idea of the problem of library schools."[2] The Memorandum, written in the latter part of 1918, after Bertram's consultation with C. C. Williamson, consists of the body of the Memorandum and seven appendices: (A) Division of cost of erected library buildings; (B) List of and general information re existing library schools; (C) Map showing geographical location of existing library schools; (D) Biographical data. Mr. C. C. Williamson; (E) Reprint of "The Need of a Plan for Library Development"; (F) Memorandum by Mr. C. C. Williamson [dated July 6, 1918]; (G) Note on the capacity of existing library schools in relation to the number of positions to be filled.

The Body of the Memorandum

After quoting the resolution of March 11, 1918, concerning the Corporation's interest in an "inquiry into the subject of schools for training librarians," Bertram defended the somewhat anomalous position of Andrew Carnegie

Bertram's Memorandum

of being "impervious to suggestions that he should subsidize existing library schools and create new ones" on the basis of Carnegie's philosophy of not believing in doing everything for an individual or a community. (His position was anomalous in that he had, by 1918, assisted four library schools.) Bertram condemned national bodies such as the American Library Association, the American Library Institute, and the League of State Librarians [League of Library Commissions?] for failure to deal effectively with the problem of training. Having thus expounded Carnegie's philosophy and condemned the agencies which might have been concerned with training problems, Bertram proceeded to consider the proposed inquiry.

The Memorandum, recognizing that an inquiry into the training facilities could be divided into two fields: one, which concerned the Corporation only generally, being that "field of library service calling for a college or a university education as the basis of the student librarian's two-year or longer library school course";[3] the other (specifically, the field of library service), being that of the small Carnegie library with a limited annual revenue of about $1,000. It identified the Corporation's concern as being training for the latter. Because of the low salaries the Memorandum acknowledged that larger libraries would attract those persons working in small libraries but reiterated that the problem was one for the library world and not Carnegie's or the Corporation's.

Aware, however, that the Corporation had expressed an interest in an inquiry into the problems of training, Bertram advised that

> Before the Trustees of this Corporation can come to any decision as to what should be done, either

particularly in the interests of Carnegie Libraries
throughout the country, or dealing with the whole
field of librarianship, a survey would require to
be made by a committee of qualified persons to
obtain a knowledge of what library training
facilities exist, to what extent those require to
be subsidized and new centers created and supported in whole or in part, and by what agencies. 4

Bertram actually was recommending a survey of library facilities as they existed, to which information relating to their need of subsidies, the need for additional facilities and support therefor might be added. The phrase, "by what agencies," suggests, however, that Bertram was not assuming that the Corporation would be the subsidizer should the study reveal the need for subsidies. Neither did he reinforce his recommendation with any of the policies proposed by Johnson in his Report . . . on the Policy of Donations to Free Public Libraries. 5

The latter part of the body of the Memorandum discusses the personnel of the committee for the proposed study. There is some confusion, however, for there are two paragraphs, one proposing a representative committee, the other identifying one man as capable of performing the study. Presumably a representative committee was favored by Williamson, for Bertram stated, "I do not agree with Mr. Williamson as to the number or composition of the committee. "6

The first paragraph, expressing Williamson's opinion, objects to charging "one person with the responsibility of such a task and to ask the Corporation to adopt a course of action based on the opinions of one man" for three reasons: (1) he "might have preconceived notions or be subjected to such influence during his investigations as to invalidate his

Bertram's Memorandum 45

conclusions"; (2) he might, through a biased or one-sided
view, offer radical proposals; (3) the problem should be
examined from the point of view "of the library profession,
library boards, state commissions and the community."
Bertram, however, rejected Williamson's proposal
and forthwith recommended Williamson as "well qualified to
take a broad view of the whole subject." As a further
recommendation, indicative of bias, Bertram added:

> He recognizes one of the fundamental troubles,
> the lack of initiative on the part of those most
> directly concerned, the librarians themselves,
> to deal with the subject of library training facil-
> ities.

The Appendices

Of the appendices, E and F bring into prominence
the figure of Charles C. Williamson. Appendix E was a
reprint of "The Need of a Plan for Library Development,"
which Bertram felt reflected his own opinions; appendix F
was a diaristic accounting of Williamson's activities at the
Saratoga Conference of the American Library Association
which he had attended in order to fulfill a mission assigned
to him by Bertram. That mission was

> Conferring with individuals in order to prepare
> a tentative list of persons who might be available
> for service on a committee to investigate and
> report on training for library work, particularly
> for the small libraries. 7

Appendix F. "Memorandum by Mr. C. C. Williamson,"
dated July 6, 1918.

From this document it is clear that Williamson
had participated in the events leading to the preparation of
the entire document transmitted to the Board of Trustees.

He confirmed that he had attended the Saratoga Conference for the purpose stated in the preceding paragraph, "to confer with individuals." The persons with whom he conferred were approached, according to Williamson, "because in most instances on account of long acquaintance with them I had confidence in their judgment and their willingness to give me their full personal opinion on any names in my list."[8]

The sixteen persons consulted, grouped according to library affiliations, represented the library schools, the American Library Association, library commissions, state libraries, public libraries, college libraries, the Library Burcau, the publisher of library indexes, and a library organizer. They are identified thus:

    Library school directors, etc.
        Sarah C. N. Bogle, Carnegie Library School
        Mary E. Hazeltine, University of Wisconsin
        Josephine L. Rathbone, Pratt Institute Library School
        E. J. Reece, New York Public Library School
        F. K. Walter, New York State Library School

    American Library Association
        George B. Utley, secretary

    Library commissions
        M. S. Dudgeon, secretary, Wisconsin Free Library Commission
        Wm. J. Hamilton, secretary, Indiana Public Library Commission

    State libraries
        W. R. Watson, State Library, New York

    Public libraries
        E. H. Anderson, director, New York Public Library
        Linda Eastman, vice-librarian, Cleveland Public Library
        Chalmers Hadley, librarian, Denver Public Library

Bertram's Memorandum   47

    College libraries
      A. S. Root, librarian, Oberlin College

    The Library Bureau
      H. R. Datz, manager

    Publisher of indexes
      H. W. Wilson

    Library organizer
      Mary E. Downey, Utah (also director of the
        Chautauqua Summer School for Librarians)[9]

Significantly absent from the list was the name of Mary E. Robbins, who had conducted the survey of library schools for the Committee on Library Training;[10] nor was there evidence of direct communication with a librarian of a small library. Of those consulted, however, the two library commissioners, the library organizer, and Miss Hazeltine, because of the interest of the Wisconsin Library School in the problems of the small library, were through daily experience in a position to know the situation in regard to small libraries. It would appear also that the limitation of the proposed study, "to investigate and report on training for library work, particularly for the small public libraries," necessarily prevented or discouraged consultation with the intellectual leaders in the field, those interested in college, university, and research library services, such as W. W. Bishop, Phineas L. Windsor, E. C. Richardson, Aksel G. S. Josephson, Adam Strohm, and others who had, since 1896, been advocating higher or graduate training for librarianship.

    Williamson recommended using a large committee, of six or seven, for the study rather than a small committee of three composed either of two librarians and one of public and educational interests, or of one librarian and two of the latter.   His reasons for the recommendations were:

> 1. The extreme difficulty (amounting almost to an impossibility) of finding one or two persons who by reason of their high standing in the profession and special qualifications for this task would be able to command the united support of library interests; but
>
> 2. Even if such a person could be found it would be difficult at any time, and especially difficult while the war lasts, for him to put aside other work and give the time and attention that would be required for a close examination of the complex situation to be reported upon, and
>
> 3. The number and variety of sectional and professional interests involved are such as to give the judgment of one librarian much less weight than the combined opinions of three or four persons looking at the questions from different viewpoints. 11

Williamson carefully defined criteria for exclusion from the committee, stating that it was deemed advisable to exclude:

> 1. Those too closely or exclusively identified with any special or narrow section of library service;
>
> 2. Anyone whose opinions seem to have so crystallized that he would not be able to make a searching and open-minded examination;
>
> 3. Those whose best work is in the past and who are therefore in danger of relying too much upon information already at hand and upon their own reputation rather than upon the thoroughness of their investigations and the cogency of their reasoning to give weight to their findings;
>
> 4. Anyone who would not be wholly acceptable to a large majority of the library profession. 12

On the basis of his conversations at Saratoga, Williamson identified the following as having been recommended by

Bertram's Memorandum

one or more persons:

Librarians

Women	Men
Sarah B. Askew	Charles Francis Dorr Belden
Zaidee Brown	William Howard Brett
Gratia Countryman	Matthew S. Dudgeon
Mary E. Downey	Chalmers Hadley
Mary F. Isom	Carl H. Milam
Lutie E. Stearns	E. R. Perry
Mary L. Titcomb	Henry N. Sanborn
Alice S. Tyler	William Richard Watson
Jessie Wells	Louis Round Wilson
	Phineas L. Windsor

Non-librarians

Dr. C. C. Certain, Detroit
Dr. Elwood Patterson Cubberly
Dr. William Davidson, supt. of schools, Pittsburgh, Pa.
Dr. John H. Finley, Albany
Dr. William Trufant Foster, Reed College
John F. Foster
Dr. James Fleming Hosic, University of Chicago
Dr. Charles R. Mann
Dr. Charles Foster Smith
Dr. Thomas, president, Middlebury College
Dr. Charles Doolittle Walcott[13]

From the list, Williamson tentatively suggested the following:

Librarians		Non-librarians
Women	Men	Davidson
		Hosic[14]
Miss Isom	Hadley	
Miss Tyler	Belden	
Miss Countryman	Windsor	
	Milam	
	Sanborn	
	Dudgeon	

And, then, narrowing the choice, Williamson stated that,

though he would prefer to inquire further before making a
final recommendation, on the basis of the present information,
he would recommend as a committee of six the following:
Miss Isom, Miss Tyler, and Messrs. Hadley, Belden,
Davidson, and Hosic.[15] He further recommended that the
proposed list "be submitted to the President and Secretary
of the American Library Association for final opinion as to
whether the selections are satisfactory to the profession."[16]

Appendix F has been analyzed in some detail because
of the insight which it provides as to Williamson's basic
approach to his assignment, his objections to a report from
three persons, his criteria for selecting persons to serve
on the committee; not, however, for its importance to the
study which was finally made. The suggestions contained in
Williamson's "Memorandum," written two days after the
Saratoga Conference, were completely ignored. Ironically
enough, in spite of Williamson's plausible objections to a
small committee, the final report is indelibly labelled as
the work of one man--C. C. Williamson himself.

Of the possible values of Williamson's Saratoga
mission two may be cited: (1) the opportunity provided him
to acquaint himself further with the problems and the personalities in the field; (2) the informal indication given to
the library profession of the interest of the Carnegie Corporation in the problem of training, for it seems unlikely
that his consultation with sixteen well-known personalities
could have gone unnoticed even among a group lacking initiative.

Appendix B. "List and General Information re Existing
Library Schools."[17]

    Attached to the report for the convenience of the

Bertram's Memorandum   51

Trustees was information on library schools which upon
examination proves to be an extraction, almost verbatim,
of the section, "Library Schools and Short Courses" from
the American Library Annual, 1916-1917 (pp. [283]-322).
No citation is made to the original source, however.

Appendix G. "Note on the Capacity of Existing Library
Schools in Relation to the Number of Positions to be Filled."

Based on a report made by Azariah Smith Root at
the 1917 Conference of the American Library Association
on "The Library School of the Future,"[18] Appendix G consists of statistics which show that library schools were preparing about 250 persons annually, training classes or apprentice classes about 500, and "others" about 200. The Appendix, after acknowledging the difficulty of determining the number of librarians and quoting the 1910 Census that there were nearly 11,000 librarians and librarian's assistants, estimated that there might be 15,000 persons engaged in library work "who do not bear the title of librarian." Unfortunately no reference was made to the number of people engaged in library work who should not have been calling themselves librarians.

The assumption of the concluding statement that "the difficulty that most libraries experience in getting sufficient librarians with adequate training may be traced directly to the lack of training facilities" was an oversimplification of the problem of staff shortages. No references were made to the following: (1) the exodus from library staff to wartime positions both for higher pay and for patriotic reasons; (2) the statement on salaries published by the Association of American Library Schools; (3) the survey of library schools undertaken by the Committee on Library Training and its almost heroic efforts to create and maintain standards; (4) the feeling by the university and college libraries that the library school programs were even then preparing especially for public library work; (5) the fact that Root had made no study of the lack of training facilities but was simply reporting on the output of librarians; (6) Root's optimistic statement made after surveying the evolutionary development of library training programs, that

> In all this there is nothing but hopefulness for the library schools; the more schools the better. There is ample room for them all and an increasing demand for the very best product they can turn out.[19]

Appointment of C. C. Williamson to Direct the Study, March 28, 1919

At the meeting of March 28, 1919, the Trustees of the Carnegie Corporation, guided by the Memorandum, approved both the undertaking of a study of training for library work and the appointment of C. C. Williamson as director of the study.[20] An Advisory Committee, composed of three, Dr. Herbert Putnam, Librarian of Congress, Dr. James H. Kirkland, Chancellor of Vanderbilt University, and Dr. Wilson Farrand, Principal of Newark Academy, was chosen.[21] Their selection represented again an ignoring of the suggestions made by Williamson, for according to his "Memorandum of July 6, 1918," he had not discussed the plan with Putnam, the only librarian of the three. Neither had he recommended at that time the appointment of any one of the three for the study.

Appointment Supported by Bertram

The appointment of C. C. Williamson to direct the

Bertram's Memorandum 53

study of Training for Library Work was almost inevitable, for in the Memorandum, Bertram had praised him as "well qualified to take a broad view of the whole subject." He indicated further that he and Williamson had discussed the problem and that Williamson's paper, "The Need of a Plan for Library Development," reflected their joint attitudes. In addition, the Trustees learned of the work of Williamson not only through his "Memorandum of July 6, 1918," but also from Appendix D which Bertram had affixed to the Memorandum. The following factual information was furnished:

Mr. C. C. Williamson

> Head of Department of Statistics and Information, Study of Methods of Americanization;[22]
>
> Graduate of Western Reserve University, Cleveland;
>
> Two years in the University of Wisconsin, including service in Library;
>
> Fellow in Economics, Columbia University;
>
> Professor of Economics and Political Science four years at Bryn Mawr College;
>
> Head of Division of Economics and Sociology, New York Public Library; Municipal Reference Library, New York City.

It was apparent from his professional record that Williamson had had no experience as a student in a library school, though he had, on occasions, lectured at the New York State Library School and at the New York Public Library School.[23] The lack of training, however, was regarded as a virtue by Edwin H. Anderson, director of the New York Public Library, who in reviewing the published report in 1924 stated:

> I do not see where they could have found a better man to make it. Dr. Williamson had an extensive university experience, both as a student and a teacher, had won an enviable reputation as a librarian, was not a product of one of the library schools, and altogether had unusual qualifications of knowledge and detachment for the task. 24

Additional Data on Williamson

Had it been necessary to convince the Trustees of Williamson's qualifications, Bertram could have appended more information concerning Williamson's association with libraries and with library schools. In a brief autobiographic sketch Williamson has related his experiences, all of which, according to him, add up to a "library career of sorts."
An early memorable experience was his service as secretary to Charles F. Thwing, president of Western Reserve University, during whose incumbency the Library School was established with Carnegie funds. Of that experience Williamson recalled:

> In later years when confronted with the fact that although without library school training myself I presumed to have opinions as to how library schools should be conducted, I sometimes countered, with tongue in cheek, that I had in effect had an informal course at Western Reserve University in the year before that school was formally opened. 25

After leaving Western Reserve University for graduate study in economics at the University of Wisconsin in 1905-06 and while working as a graduate assistant for Professor Richard T. Ely, he recataloged Ely's private library, cataloged and classified a collection of pamphlets, clippings, etc., and selected books in economics to strengthen the

Bertram's Memorandum 55

collections of the University of Wisconsin and the State Historical Society.

He accepted a more remunerative fellowship at Columbia University in 1906 and by 1907 had received a degree in economics. Three positions were available to him upon graduation: (1) Executive Secretary of Western Reserve University and instructor in Political Science; (2) Reference librarian in the Cleveland Public Library; (3) Associate in Economics at Bryn Mawr College. Having chosen the last named, he remained at Bryn Mawr until he was invited to organize a department of Economics in the New York Public Library. For that appointment, beginning May 1911, he had been recommended by E. R. A. Seligman, Economics professor at Columbia University, and W. D. Johnston, librarian of Columbia University. In 1914 he was transferred to the Municipal Reference Library where he remained until his resignation on May 1, 1918, to become statistician for the Carnegie Study of Methods of Americanization. In October of that same year he not only continued with the Carnegie appointment but also agreed to resume the headship of the Economics Division of the New York Public Library, a position made vacant by the resignation of Adelaide R. Hasse.

When to these responsibilities was added that of the study on Training for Library work, it could have been expected that there would be a delay in the completion of the study but not necessarily in its planning.

Williamson's Notes Prepared for the Advisory Committee, April 28, 1920

At the first of two meetings[26] held by the Advisory Committee, on April 28, 1920, Williamson, a year after his appointment, presented a document, "Notes on the Aims, Scope and Method of the Study of Training for Library Service," prepared for the Committee.[27] In the document Williamson identified the objects of the Study of Training for Library Work as being:

> 1. To aid the Corporation in the formation of its own future policy with respect to training for librarianship in general and specifically in respect to existing subsidies and pending requests for aid in establishing other schools.
>
> 2. To improve library service by presenting to the public and to the library profession a clear analysis of the problem of providing an adequately trained personnel for all kinds and grades of library service, and to suggest plans of development to be adopted by public authorities, educational institutions and professional organizations.[28]

That Williamson accepted the scope as being the study of all types of training agencies is evident, for he stated:

> It does not seem worthwhile or even possible to make an intensive study of the schools without paying attention also to the training classes, apprentice courses, college, university and normal school courses in library economy, summer schools, correspondence instruction, institutes, etc. As a matter of fact, for the solution of the training problem which confronts the small public library it will probably be necessary to rely primarily not on the "schools" but on some other type of training.[29]

Williamson further identified the proposed study as a "piece of pioneer work" after acknowledging that certain aspects of the training question had been touched upon by the Committee on Library Training and the Professional Training Section of the American Library Association and that both the Library Department and the Secondary Education Department of the National Education Association had

Bertram's Memorandum 57

undertaken studies of school library work. He emphasized, however, that "no one has ventured to envisage as a whole the problem of training for all kinds of library work." The method of study outlined by Williamson involved: (1) conferences and correspondence with persons, the result of which would produce questions for discussion with individuals and interested groups; and (2) the conventional questionnaire when necessary. Appended to the document were tentative plans for pursuing the study of (1) library schools; (2) training classes; (3) school librarians; (4) normal schools; (5) colleges and universities; (6) summer schools; (7) correspondence courses; (8) the problem in New York City.

The "Notes" concluded with some working hypotheses which had evolved during the preliminary planning. Williamson identified these as needs for: (1) definition and standardization in respect to training methods and agencies; (2) raising minimum standards; (3) an accrediting process to be carried on continuously; (3) formulation of definitions and minimum standards for other kinds of training agencies, such as training classes, summer school courses, etc.; (5) some central accrediting body; (6) coordination of the facilities of the schools and other training agencies in some way; (7) formulation of minimum standards for general courses in cataloguing, book selection, reference work, classification, work with children, etc. The values of such standardization were anticipated as being:
 (a) a freer interchange of credits among accredited agencies,
 (b) the possibility of meeting requirements for certificate or promotion while in service or without extended absence.[31]

Williamson emphasized that the special value of the latter was that it would offer an opportunity for librarians of small-town libraries to receive some training for their positions.

The sustained impact of these convictions on Williamson and the relevance of these needs to his proposed solutions can be seen both in his analysis of the current scene and in his recommendations to be made later to the Carnegie Corporation.

Approval of Plan by the Advisory Committee

That the Advisory Committee approved the plan submitted by Williamson is indicated in Williamson's report to the Carnegie Corporation in which he stated:

> An outline of the scope and method of the study laid before the [Advisory] committee and discussed at that time [April 28, 1920] has been followed in the main. 32

As further clarification, Williamson added:

> It was found to be necessary, however, to limit the scope of the original by confining attention largely to the so-called professional library schools--fifteen in number--and dealing only incidentally with training classes, summer schools, and other types of training agencies. 33

It had presumably been Williamson's idea originally to "envisage as a whole the problem of training for all kinds of library work," for in referring to the scope of the study he had stated in 1920:

> The phraseology of the resolutions adopted by the Corporation might be interpreted narrowly to confine the study to the thirteen or fourteen so-called "library schools," and such limited inquiry might be of some value, but it has seemed much wiser on the whole to interpret the resolutions more broadly and include other training agencies. 34

Bertram's Memorandum

As if associating the study with his earlier analysis of "The Need of a Plan for Library Development," Williamson added:

> For the solution of the training problem which confronts the small public library it will probably be necessary to rely primarily not on the 'schools' but on some other type of training.[35]

Effect of the change in scope. -- Though the scope of the study was limited, the first objective, defined by Williamson on April 28, 1920, remained constant, that being to "aid the Corporation in the formation of its own future policy" concerning training for librarianship. Objective two, the improvement of library service and the suggestion of plans of development, was necessarily limited when the only type of training program lengthily examined was that of the library schools.

Before discussing the preparation and content of the report further, references will be made to some of Williamson's activities and to some of the concepts which guided him in the preparation of the report. The period to be examined covers the dates between his appointment to direct the study, March 28, 1919, and the presentation of the formal report to the Carnegie Corporation by the Advisory Committee on March 23, 1922.

Notes

1. The Trustees in 1918 were: Andrew Carnegie, president; James Bertram, Robert A. Franks, John A. Poynton, Henry S. Pritchett, Charles L. Taylor, Robert S. Woodward, and Elihu Root as an ex-officio member. Robert M. Lester, Forty Years of Carnegie Giving (New York: Charles Scribner's Sons, 1941), p. 64.

2. Carnegie Corporation of New York, Memorandum, p. 6.

3. Ibid., p. 3.

4.   Ibid., p. 5.

5.   For information on the Report . . . on the Policy of Donations by Alvin S. Johnson see p. 18-22.

6.   Carnegie Corporation of New York, Memorandum, p. 6.

7.   Carnegie Corporation of New York, Memorandum, "Appendix F," p. 1.

8.   Ibid.

9.   Ibid.

10.   Letter from Azariah Smith Root, February 6, 1914 (in the files of the Oberlin College Library); "Robbins, Mary Esther," Library Journal, XXXVIII (June, 1913), 378.

11.   Carnegie Corporation of New York, Memorandum, "Appendix F," p. 1-2.

12.   Ibid., p. 2.

13.   Ibid.

14.   Ibid., p. 3.

15.   Ibid.

16.   Ibid.

17.   Carnegie Corporation of New York, Memorandum, "Appendix B," p. 1-6.

18.   Azariah S. Root, "The Library School of the Future," A. L. A. Bulletin XI (July, 1917), 157-160.

19.   Ibid., p. 157.

Bertram's Memorandum   61

20. Williamson II, p. v.

21. Ibid.

22. The immediate association of Williamson with the
Study of Methods of Americanization was significant in
view of the sponsorship of that Study by the Carnegie
Corporation of New York. The following announcement
appeared in Library Journal:
> The Carnegie Corporation of New York has
> undertaken to finance a study of the existing
> methods by which Americanization is being
> fostered in this country, so that the various
> agencies which have arisen in the last twenty-
> five years, together with other older influence
> and experience potent in uniting the foreign with
> the native born, may be joined in common aims
> and efforts for the general welfare. . . .
>
> Of interest to librarians is the announcement
> that Dr. C. C. Williamson, the librarian in
> charge of the Municipal Reference Library in
> New York City and President of the Special
> Libraries Association, has been appointed
> statistician for the survey.

"Carnegie Corporation to Study Americanization," LJ, XLIII
(May, 1918), 339.

23. "New York State Library School," LJ, XL (March,
1915), 190. He gave a similar lecture at the New York
Public Library School on "Municipal Library Reference
Work." "Library School of the New York Public Library,"
LJ, XL (April, 1915), 276. See also LJ, XXXVI (Jan.,
1912), 37.

Of his lectures at the New York Public Library
School, Williamson reminisced in 1955:
> At the same time I was organizing my new
> department [at the New York Public Library]
> Miss Plummer was organizing the new Library
> School for which Mr. Carnegie had provided
> the funds. I cooperated with her by giving her
> students practice work and even gave some
> lectures to her class, but I am afraid I always
> had a rather dim view of the nature and quality

of the instruction in that school, including especially my own little part in it. Williamson, Statement, June, 1955, p. 12.

24. Edwin H. Anderson, "Training for Library Service," LJ, XLIX (May 15, 1924), 462.

25. Williamson, Statement, June, 1955, p. 9.

26. The second meeting was held on February 3, 1922, after completion of the study. Letter to the Carnegie Corporation from Herbert Putnam (In Re: Survey by Dr. C. C. Williamson of Training for Library Work), March 23, 1922.

27. C. C. Williamson, "Notes on the Aims, Scope and Method of the Study of Training for Library Service, for Discussion at the Meeting of the Advisory Committee, to be held Wednesday, April 28, 1920." (Typewritten copy, marked "Confidential," in the files of C. C. Williamson). 16 p.

28. Ibid., p. 3. The objectives as defined in "Notes" differs from that for which Williamson undertook the Saratoga mission, to secure the names of persons who would be available to serve on a committee "to investigate and report on training for library work, particularly for the small public libraries." (Italics mine.) Objective one is in keeping with Bertram's recognition in his Memorandum of 1918 that the Board of Trustees would sooner or later be called upon to deal with the problem of library schools and that he, through the Memorandum and the accompanying papers, was offering some statement of the case.

29. Williamson, "Notes," p. 4.

30. Ibid., p. 14-16.

31. Ibid., p. 16.

32. Williamson I, p. 5.

33. Ibid.
34. Williamson, "Notes," p. 3-4.
35. Ibid., p. 4.

Chapter 3

Williamson and the Preparation of the Report

Though Williamson had agreed to direct the study, he accepted with the understanding that he could not begin until he had completed his assignment as statistician for the Study of Americanization. He was not, however, during that period of completion, isolated from the newly assumed responsibility, for he was stating his concern over the poverty of the schools and his opinion on the need of training before the meeting of the Advisory Committee of April 28, 1920.

<u>Letter to William F. Yust, January 3, 1920.</u> -- Upon learning that William F. Yust had been appointed chairman of a committee of alumni of the New York State Library School, organized to present the case for more adequate salaries and financial support for the School, Williamson wrote:

> I cannot help feeling apprehensive that unless salaries are materially increased the school will not long be able to attract or retain the services of men and women who, on account of their professional achievements, personality and teaching ability, should be found on the staff of the oldest and most successful of the library schools. [1]

He expressed approval of the committee's work, noting that

> Of all the professional schools supported by this or any other state, I do not know of any that has produced larger returns in public service for the money invested in it. [2]

More prophetically the letter contained an acknowledg-

Preparation of the Report 65

ment from Williamson that library training was necessary and for that statement alone it is important. After stating that he had entered the library field from the teaching profession, he admitted:

> For some years I was inclined to question the necessity or value of such training for the particular kind of specialized work in which I had been interested, but an experience of nearly ten years has thoroughly changed my attitude towards library school training.³

He added further: "I find myself more and more reluctant to consider the appointment of any person who has not had the training offered by a good library school."⁴

Williamson expressed his conviction on the need of training again in a speech, made in June, after the meeting of the Advisory Committee, in which he viewed Carnegie's contribution to the public library movement.

Williamson's Appraisal of Carnegie Contributions, 1920

Soon after the meeting with the Advisory Committee on April 28, 1920, Williamson was invited to make the Founder's Day speech on June 15, 1920, at Western Reserve University Library School. It was in that speech, "Andrew Carnegie: His Contribution to the Public Library Movement," rather than in his earlier "The Need of a Plan for Library Development," that Williamson acknowledged that the proliferation of small Carnegie buildings had been a factor in ineffectual service and emphasized that effective service was dependent on "library workers of the highest order of ability and the most thorough training."⁵

Williamson's acknowledgment was a belated recognition of the conclusion of the Johnson Report and, to some extent, a contradiction of his earlier ideas.⁶ As such it marked a direct change in Williamson's attitude toward the problem of training for librarians of small libraries. In the speech he viewed critically the impact of the Carnegie donations on communities and frankly stated that Carnegie had "done more to promote free libraries in the higher sense through these library schools [i. e. Western Reserve, the New York Public Library School, the Carnegie Library School of Pittsburgh, and the Carnegie Library School of Atlanta] than through any like expenditure of money for buildings."7

The latter statement was the first evaluative statement, made publicly, 8 by anyone associated with the Carnegie Corporation, of the importance of library schools in helping to fulfill the purpose of the establishment of library buildings. It was momentous when issuing from the director of the Carnegie study, for though he promised his listeners nothing, his insistence on the need for "library workers of the highest ability and the most thorough training" presaged the content of the recommendations of the final report.

Though recognizing the philanthropic motivation which had prompted Carnegie to contribute libraries "as the best agencies for improving the mass of the people because they only help those who help themselves,"9 Williamson observed:

> There is no use denying that in some cases the gift of a building has actually deprived a community for the time being of a library service, by putting it to sleep with the opiate of self-congratulations and self-satisfaction in the possession of a fitting library structure. 10

Praising rather than disparaging Carnegie's philanthropic principle, Williamson asked despite his reference to the "opiate of self-congratulations":

> Can anyone doubt that on the whole the one contribution best calculated eventually to awaken and

Preparation of the Report 67

sustain the community's interest in such a service is the building?[11]

Williamson placed greater emphasis, however, on the responsibilities of providing better service for the buildings so generously given. For the accomplishment of that better service he predicted that

> More library buildings will be needed and far greater expenditure for books; but more than all will be required better training and more adequate salaries for librarianship, which will mean greater skill in so organizing the world of print as to bring to each individual that small part he can use to the best advantage.[12]

Acknowledging that Carnegie had said little about the function of the librarian, Williamson attempted to show that Carnegie would not "overlook the importance of skill and efficiency in every kind of library service." He quoted from a speech made by Carnegie in dedicating the library building at Braddock, Pennsylvania. Speaking to the working-men gathered there, Carnegie had said:

> Knowledge is now so various, so extensive, so minute, that it is impossible for any man to know thoroughly more than one small branch. This is the age of the specialist, therefore you who have to make your living in this world should resolve to know the art which gives you support; to know that thoroughly and well, to be an expert in your specialty.[13]

In adapting the advice to librarianship, Williamson observed:

> Mr. Carnegie was too shrewd not to see that before the chemist can go to the public library and read the last word on his specialty, the librarian must see that the library has the last word and that there shall be no fumbling and lost motion in getting it to the busy specialist.[14]

Not only did Williamson emphasize the need of thorough training, he warned that

> There is an unfortunate and altogether erroneous idea in many minds that a person of average in-

telligence and education can step into a library and give efficient service. It is quite usual for applicants for library positions cheerfully to admit that they have neither training nor experience, but that they consider themselves fitted for the work because they have used library books![15]

This was the attitude, perhaps unknown at the time to Williamson, that Andrew Carnegie had reflected when he wrote to Melvil Dewey in 1890.[16]

Williamson, while making no attempt to offer recommendations to the Corporation, concluded his speech by saying:

> In the years since Mr. Carnegie began his library benefactions it has become increasingly clear that no influence is so potent in awakening a community's interest in a library service and in stimulating it to levy taxes to pay for it, as the presence of a properly qualified and trained librarian.[17]

Later reference by Williamson to his Western Reserve speech. -- Williamson referred to his speech in his "Summary of Report on Training for Library Work," wherein he took the liberty of stating why he felt that it would be a "wise policy for the Carnegie Corporation to adopt a program of aiding in the promotion of public library service through training and other practicable methods."[18] He spoke more critically, however, in his "Summary of Report," than he had at Western Reserve, for his audience in 1921 was the Carnegie Corporation. In evaluating the philanthropic grants he wrote:

> Aside from buildings and an occasional endowment, little thought or money has been put into the development of this agency of community and individual welfare. It is possible, moreover, that buildings and endowments are among the least desirable forms for private philanthropy to take.[19]

Preparation of the Report 69

He then informed the Trustees that
> Some phases of this question were discussed by the writer in an address on Mr. Carnegie's library philanthropies delivered to the Western Reserve University Library School, which is available in print and can therefore be merely referred to here. [20]

The recommendation ultimately made by Williamson to the Corporation, that it might aid in the promotion of library service through aiding in the training of librarians, would seem to be appropriate even when viewed in relation to his Western Reserve address alone. From those statements which he had made on June 15, 1920, one could readily conclude that Williamson would have advocated, should an opportunity have arisen, that the Corporation allocate funds for the education of librarians. [21]

Two Concepts of Williamson

Immediately after his appointment to direct the Carnegie study, Williamson was catapulted into a position of prominence in the American Library Association, both by his contributions at the Asbury Park Conference of June, 1919, and by his sustained interest in a program of certification throughout the preparation of the study. Not only was he appointed a member of Council for a five year period, [22] he delivered two speeches in 1919, one on "A Look Ahead for the Small Library";[23] the other, "Some Present-Day Aspects of Library Training."[24] Within these speeches are found two concepts which guided, or were present in, the preparation of the report. These concepts related to county library work and certification.

Concept of County Library Work

In his first speech, "The Need of a Plan for

Library Development" the individual librarian of the small library bore the brunt of the scathing attack because of his assumption that "an efficient librarian will stimulate interest; therefore I maintain that the librarian is the proper point of attack. " In his second examination of the needs of the small library Williamson had apparently re-examined the situation and was admitting that "most libraries are too small to be administratively and economically efficient."[25]

He made that statement in a speech to the League of Library Commissions on June 25, 1919; in it he further deprecated the small library by adding:

> It seems to me that the average small library in most states is an anachronism and a survival, in a class with the ungraded and unsupervised district school.[26]

In defining the needs of library service as three: (1) the need of a trained personnel; (2) the need of cooperation and some degree of centralization; (3) the need for standards of service, Williamson elaborated on the need for centralization and cooperation. For the first time he referred to county library work and acknowledged:

> I fancy we face an uphill task in bringing local boards and librarians to realize that their opportunity for usefulness depends to a great extent on giving up some of their precious independence. If they could see the situation as an outsider sees it, the small libraries in every state would become ardent champions of county systems and strong commissions, instead of looking with suspicion and jealousy on what seems to them an unwarranted encroachment on local autonomy.[27]

Reiterating his opinion he added:

> The outlook for small libraries seems so entirely dependent on the work of commissions, county systems, and improved state laws, that mere enlightened self-interest ought to lead them to organize a movement for library extension

Preparation of the Reports 71

that would convince members of the legislature
of its vital importance. 28

Though the issue of county library work was not the
main theme of the speech given to the League of Library
Commissions, its inclusion indicated that by June, 1919,
Williamson had been considering the merits of larger units
of library service as a solution to the problems of the small
library. His belief in the concept of county library service
was strengthened during his preparation of the report, for
in it he expressed again his thoughts of 1919:

> What can be done for communities too small or
> too poor to avail themselves of a professionally
> trained librarian? There is but one satisfactory
> answer: make the library unit large enough and
> efficient service is possible. This may be done
> through the county system. 29

Concept of Certification

Though Williamson had in 1918 proposed the creation
of some central organization to coordinate the various training programs to be offered to librarians of small libraries,
he had, by 1919, conceived the idea of a more powerful
central organization, one which would organize training,
formulate standards, and certify librarians. It was in a
speech delivered at the Asbury Park Conference that Williamson proposed the establishment of an American Library
Association Training Board "for organizing training, formulating standards and certifying library workers."30

The significance of the speech made at Asbury Park
in relation to Williamson's final report on library training
may be seen in its inclusion in the appendix of the unpub-

lished report and Williamson's statement that his proposal for a training board

> grew out of the initial consideration given to the present study of training for library work. From his general knowledge of the situation and his preliminary investigations, the writer became convinced that the primary need in any plan for improving library service and training facilities is some adequate and appropriate agency for formulating and applying standards, not only for the library schools but for other training agencies and for all persons engaged in library work. 31

Other Evidences of Williamson's Continuing Interest

Prior to Williamson's appointment to direct the Carnegie study he had been appointed a member of the Committee of Five of the American Library Association "to make a general survey of American library service in view of the post-war conditions of readjustment," by the Executive Board at its meeting of January 11, 1919. 32 In the distribution of duties among the committee members Williamson was assigned the division

> embracing the formation, training, control and welfare of the library staff [which] will include education and training; employment problems, such as selection, civil service control, efficiency ratings, promotion and discipline; salaries, grades and certification; welfare problems, working conditions, hours, vacations, pensions, staff associations and unions; and problems of status, especially those affecting the academic rank of librarians in educational institutions with the rating of the library as compared with other departments of a school or college. 33

The comprehensive scope of Williamson's assignment on the Committee of Five, in addition to his later appointment to direct the Carnegie study, focused his attention increasingly on the problem of training. His discussion at

Preparation of the Report   73

the Asbury Park Conference, wherein he made his proposal
for a training board, was not in itself surprising or unexpected evidence of his concern. What might be regarded
as questionable procedure was Williamson's prefatory remark
that since the President of the American Library Association,
William Warner Bishop, had asked him to discuss the topic
before he knew of his responsibilities on the Committee of
Five, he had not shared his views with the other committee
members but chose rather to speak as an individual. By
such a decision the idea of the training board emerged as
eminently his rather than the Committee's.

Williamson's appointment in 1919 to the Special
Committee of Five on Standardization, Certification and
Library Training, which recommended

> That a National Board of Certification for Li-
> brarians be established by the American Library
> Association and that permanent provision for
> such a Board be incorporated in the constitution
> of the Association, [34]

identified him readily as an active proponent of certification.

<u>Williamson as chairman of the A. L. A. Committee on
National Certification.</u> -- Williamson's later appointment as
chairman of the committee to be known as the Committee
on National Certification and the comprehensive report made
at the Swampscott Conference on June 21, 1921,[35] imply a
continuing absorption[36] in the problems of certification. In
the Committee report appeared an "Outline of a Tentative
Scheme" of certification which embraced four classes of
certificates. For each class the educational requirements,
the experience, and the types of positions were clearly defined. The emphasis on training was evident in the educational requirement for Class I and Grade A of Classes II
and III which stated:

Education: (1) Graduation from an approved college with reading knowledge of at least one modern language other than English; and (2) not less than one year's successful study in an approved library school with recommendation of school faculty. [37]

Though the 1921 report of the Committee on National Certification was prepared after Williamson's visit to the library schools and before his report was written for the Carnegie Corporation, neither the library schools[38] nor the practicing librarians could have been totally unaware that his final conclusions would be that a college degree should be a prerequisite for admission to library schools and that library schools should offer general professional training in a one year's course.

Response of the American Library Association to the Committee Report. -- Williamson was no doubt encouraged by the reaction at the Swampscott Conference to the report of his Committee on National Certification, if not altogether pleased, for the Council voted that the report be accepted and that the Committee be continued "to give the subject continuous consideration and to report [to the Council] at the midwinter conference."[39]

During the latter part of the year, while writing the Corporation report, Williamson and his Committee formulated resolutions for presentation at the ensuing meeting. The resolutions, published in *Library Journal*, December 15, 1921, optimistically anticipated the acceptance of a plan for voluntary certification of librarians.[40] However, at the midwinter meeting strong opposition to the plan of certification manifested itself, objections being voiced by a member of Williamson's committee, Phineas L. Windsor. After an exchange of points of view, the Association voted

To recommit the resolution to the existing com-

Preparation of the Report   75

mittee with direction that it formulate standards
of certification and provisions which are to be
recommended for incorporation into state laws
and to suggest methods by which the Association
can cooperate in securing proper legislation. 41

Thus was Williamson's concept of a certification plan rejected, a plan which he had been perfecting since the original proposal in 1919. Following the midwinter meeting, which he had not attended, Williamson resigned as chairman of the Committee and at the Detroit Conference of 1922 no report was made.

The Carnegie Report

Having presented his plans and having received the approval of the Advisory Committee on April 28, 1920, to pursue them, Williamson, during the summer of 1920, made preliminary inquiries and prepared an outline of the topics about which he wished to secure information from library school officials and teachers. 42 Though Williamson did not include in his report on "Training for Library Work" those topics in which he was interested, the completed report indicates that he was guided by the "Notes" which he had included in his explanation of the study for the Advisory Committee.

While he had stated that "no detailed outline has been prepared for the treatment of library schools," he had suggested that the following features required attention:

> Kinds of work for which school training is needed (Very little attention need be given to their origin and history.)
>
> Source and character of students--methods of recruiting.
>
> Entrance requirements--character of examinations

--lack of uniformity--admission by credit.

Grading and classification of students.

Analysis of curricula--what subjects should be taught and in what proportion the first year? The second year? Do the schools keep abreast of the best thought and practice?

Teaching staff.

Methods of instruction--effectiveness--compared with other kinds of professional instruction. Character and value of practice work.

Finances and administration.

Placement of students--number remaining in library work - their earning and success.

Is the school doing all it should to meet the training needs of its natural territory?

Can and should the schools offer specialized courses?

How can the demand for more advanced instruction be provided for?

How can properly trained teachers be provided?[43]

Schools visited. -- Williamson visited the schools in which he held conferences with the principals and directors. His itinerary may be followed through consulting the reports of the various schools, for example, he visited the New York State Library School on November 22, 1920;[44] Simmons College on November 23;[45] the St. Louis Library School on January 6, 1921;[46] the Carnegie Library School of Atlanta on May 9 and 10, 1921.[47]

The fifteen library schools visited and included in the study may be identified as follows:

Preparation of the Report　　　　　　　　　77

Code number in Williamson II p. 73	Name of School
1	New York State Library School, Albany, N. Y.
2	Pratt Institute School of Library Science, Brooklyn, N. Y.
3	University of Illinois Library School, Urbana, Ill.
4	Carnegie Library School, Pittsburgh, Pa.
5	Simmons College School of Library Science, Boston, Mass.
6	Library School of Western Reserve University, Cleveland
7	Library School, Carnegie Library of Atlanta
8	Library School of the University of Wisconsin
9	Library School of the New York Public Library
10	Library School, University of Washington
11	Library School of the Los Angeles Public Library
12	St. Louis Library School, St. Louis, Mo.
13	University of California courses in Library Science, Berkeley, Calif.
	Riverside Library Service School
	Syracuse University Library School[48]

Of the schools as a group Williamson reported:

All except three or four of the fifteen schools covered in this report began as training classes for some particular library. In order to admit students from other libraries they were transformed into library schools. The transformation, however, has not in every case been fully accomplished. Many of the schools, as is pointed

out at various points in later chapters, still
exhibit some of the characteristics of training
schools, much as a college may which has developed from a secondary school by changing its
name, adding a new instructor or so, and lengthening the course, without making substantial
change of personnel or equipment. 49

The portions of the resultant report, including facts which could have been secured only through direct interview or observation, are a tribute not only to the skill of Williamson in eliciting information but also to the cooperative spirit of the schools which accepted Williamson as a representative of the Carnegie Corporation. Williamson, however, was not particularly impressed with the persons whom he interviewed or met, for he concluded:

It is to the library schools that we should be
able to turn for inspiration and guidance, but it
must be confessed that trained leadership of the
quality now demanded is not likely to be produced
by the present curriculum and personnel of the
professional schools. 50

Completion of the report. -- Though Williamson completed his visits to the schools by May 1921, he was delayed in the writing of the report, just as he had been in the undertaking of the report, by an additional responsibility, the acceptance of a new position on June 1, 1921, as Director of Information Service of the Rockefeller Foundation. 51 It was not until later in the year that he organized the material, presumably after the report of the Committee on National Certification, presented at the Swampscott Conference, had been written, for he referred optimistically to the Certification report in the chapter on "Standardization and Certification." At that time he wrote:

A plan for voluntary national certification has,
therefore, been worked out in the last two years
and <u>accepted in principle by the American Library
Association.</u> 52 (Italics mine).

Preparation of the Report 79

On the basis of the statement that the plan had been accepted in principle it would appear that the report could only have been written after the Swampscott Conference and before the Chicago Midwinter meeting when the plan initiated by Williamson as chairman of the A. L. A. Committee on National Certification was rejected. [53]

At the request of James Bertram, Williamson condensed the report for the convenience of the Trustees of the Carnegie Corporation, extracting only the most pertinent data and the recommendations which he ventured to offer. Before the report could be submitted to the Corporation, however, Williamson submitted both the report and the summary to the Advisory Committee.

Approval by the Advisory Committee

The Advisory Committee met on February 3, 1922, [54] at which time the general features, the conclusions, and the recommendations of Williamson's report were discussed. Having viewed the report critically the Committee informed the Corporation that it found itself in complete agreement as follows:

> (1) That the Survey had been appropriate and thorough;
>
> (2) That the Report embodies useful information, much of it novel, and a discerning analysis of the strength and weakness in the existing systems of training which make the Report in itself a valuable contribution. The publication of the general portions of it (that is to say, all except those dealing with particular library schools) would, in the judgment of the Committee, be highly desirable;
>
> (3) As to both the conclusions and recommendations regarding particular library schools, the

Committee assumes that it is concerned only
with the general questions involved.

(4) With the general conclusions the Committee
finds itself in hearty agreement. It especially
commends and supports these two general conclusions:

<u>a</u>: That, as to the schools, the present
need is not the further multiplication of library
schools or diffusion of grants in aid of them,
but the concentration of aid in grants to a few
selected schools;

<u>b</u>: That even in the interest of the service
in the smaller libraries, the most effective
grants (apart from the creation of demonstration
units) may prove to be those tending to raise the
general standards of the Library profession and
render definite the qualifications.

(5) With the general recommendations underscored in the Summary accompanying the Report,
the Committee also agrees: and this will include
all through page 11 of that Summary, leaving
only (as outside of the responsibility of the Committee) the recommendations touching particular
schools, beginning with that at New York City. [55]

Thus, the Advisory Committee officially informed the Corporation of its approval of Williamson's survey of "Training for Library Work." The Committee further approved Williamson's opinion that estimates should not accompany the recommendations since "without knowledge of the disposition of the Corporation towards the projects outlined, [the estimates] might be premature."[56] On March 30, 1922, Williamson was informed by Herbert Putnam,[57] member of the Committee, that the favorable report of the Advisory Committee, dated March 23, 1922, had been forwarded to the Corporation.

Preparation of the Report   81

The Complete Report Reviewed

Williamson's Sustained Concepts

Williamson's report must be viewed as one man's analysis of the problems and plan for library training, despite his own earlier advice that the study be undertaken by a qualified committee none of whom should have opinions "so crystallized that he would not be able to make a searching and open-minded investigation."[58] To the extent that Williamson had formulated his concepts on certification, correspondence courses, and county work prior to his actually beginning the study, his own ideas were crystallized.

On certification. -- The report was inextricably interwoven with Williamson's all-encompassing concern for a plan of certification, a concern evident immediately from the chapter on "Types of Library Work and Training." This was a summary, in part, of the 1921 Report of the A. L. A. Committee on National Certification, of which Williamson was chairman. The relevancy and relationship were emphasized further by the inclusion, in the unpublished version, of that Report of the A. L. A. Committee. In both Williamson attempted to define levels of professional and clerical work, associating with each an educational attainment. In the chapter on "Types of Library Work and Training," he summarized the educational distinctions as follows:

> Two main types of training for library work are required. The first is the broad general education represented at its minimum by a full college course which has included certain important subjects, plus at least one year's graduate study in a library school properly organized to give a thorough preparation for the kind of service we describe as 'professional.' The second type calls for a general education represented approximately by a high school course followed by a course of instruction designed to give a good understanding of

> the mechanics and routine operations of the library, together with sufficient instruction and practice to insure proficiency and skill in one or more kinds of clerical and routine work which we may call 'sub-professional' or 'clerical.'[59]

Williamson also related the Corporation report to the work of the Committee on National Certification in the chapter, "Standardization and Certification." After dismissing the Association of American Library Schools as a demonstrably weak agency for determining standards because it was "helpless, either to enforce existing inadequate requirements or to make necessary advances,"[60] he reviewed the progress made in regard to certification by the American Library Association, including therein references to the Committee report.

He identified the functions of a proposed National Certification Board as including the exercising of a degree of supervision over both the library schools and training classes and assumed that

> To a greater or less extent it would take the place of the Association of American Library Schools, which, as has been pointed out, cannot be relied upon to become an effective instrument for enforcing minimum standards on the part of library schools.[61]

He stated further:

> The power of the Board to withhold the national professional certificate from the graduates of an unaccredited school would make its rulings and decisions effective. The board should not stop, however, with merely formulating standards and inspecting and accrediting training agencies, and then certifying the output of accredited institutions or admitting to certificate by examination. It should also become a central agency for promoting professional training in the many ways that would be open to it. It should very soon occupy a place analogous to that of the Council on Medical Education of the American Medical Association.[62]

Preparation of the Report

Within the brief "Summary of Report," digested especially for the Trustees, Williamson expressed again his sustained conviction that

> Fundamental to the problem of raising standards of professional training is the need for a system of professional certificates and some properly constituted body for accrediting training agencies. [63]

He also informed the Trustees that "the value and possible question of a national certification board are pointed out throughout the report."[64] (Italics mine). Williamson further advised the Trustees that the publication of the report itself might assist in crystallizing sentiment for such an agency. Finally, in anticipation of the financial needs of such an agency, should one be established, he recommended:

> that the Carnegie Corporation should be ready to give aid whenever a concrete proposal is presented with the endorsement of the library profession.[65]

On correspondence courses. -- Williamson had, since 1918, when he had written "The Need of a Plan for Library Development," manifested a continuing interest in correspondence courses, an interest which had not been extinguished when he prepared the Corporation report. Two chapters of the report, "Training in Service" and "Correspondence Instruction," were more specifically related to his 1918 concept than were other chapters, for in them he reiterated his belief in correspondence courses.

He hypothesized further that the failure of the profession to make use of the correspondence method of instruction illustrated the general backwardness both in the development of library services and in technical training. Once again, as he had done in 1918, he scored librarians for their essential conservatism and lack of initiative. He appeared convinced that

long overworked and underpaid, submerged in
routine duties and free from a strong public
demand for efficiency, librarians as a whole have
not themselves been innovators nor are they in
general inclined to experiment with new ideas.[66]

He viewed with some satisfaction reports of correspondence courses at the University of Chicago, which was offering twenty-four lessons on "Technical Methods of Library Science";[67] at the California State Library, which was offering correspondence instruction in cataloging; and at the University of Wisconsin, which offered through its Extension Division in 1920 a course to between 250 and 300 students.[68]

So convinced was he of the efficacy of correspondence instruction that he specifically suggested that the proposed Library School to be established in New York City offer correspondence courses.[69] He included also, as one of the reasons for allocating money for a textbook project, the need of proper texts for that instruction.[70] His recognition of the need of textbooks was, however, more comprehensive in scope, for he advised the Corporation:

> In my judgment a very important contribution
> could be made at this time to the improvement
> of instruction in library schools by a comparatively
> small amount of money used to stimulate the
> preparation of text-books and manuals adapted
> for instructional purposes. On the faculties of
> library schools are a few men and women who
> have been hoping for years to have an opportunity
> to put into shape for publication the results of
> their study and experience in a special field.
> Teaching schedules are heavy, however, and not
> many library schools can afford to give their
> instructors sabbatical years. I would therefore
> recommend that the Carnegie Corporation appropriate for a period of years a sum of money
> large enough to pay the salary, and perhaps an
> allowance for traveling expenses, of one library
> school instructor on leave of absence each year
> for the specific purpose of enabling him to com-

Preparation of the Report   85

plete for publication a work which when published
will be useful to the schools and to the library
profession generally. [71]

Williamson regarded correspondence instruction,
finally, as a means of furthering the development of a
national certification plan since, through taking correspondence courses, library workers would have been able to
qualify for certification. [72]

On county library work. -- Though Williamson had
not referred to county library work until June, 1919, in his
speech before the League of Library Commissions, he was,
by 1921, asserting that only through adopting larger units of
service could small communities hope to employ professionally
qualified librarians. [73] In the report, as he had done in
"The Need of a Plan for Library Development," he again
deplored the inadequate services being offered in small libraries, affirming that

> Little libraries in the hands of uneducated and
> untrained, often unpaid, librarians offer as hopeless a situation as can be found in the whole
> range of social and educational problems. [74]

Other references in the Report. -- In discussing
specialization for second year training, Williamson proposed
in the published report that the University of California
offer a course in county library work. [75] Such a suggestion
appears arbitrary until the deleted sections of the full report
furnish information concerning Williamson's interest in the
county library programs of Oregon and California. Not only
did Williamson express admiration for the idea; he recommended to the Carnegie Corporation that it promote the
concept of county library service.

Omitted from the published report are his two
recommendations relating (1) to a study of the county library

systems of Oregon and California and (2) to the fostering of demonstration units of county library service. The deleted section reads:

> By means of the county system a library service as good as the best to be found in any city can be provided for every individual in a territory covering thousands of square miles. Moreover, by reason of good roads, telephones, and parcel post, this can be done almost as economically as in populous centers.
>
> In library circles there is much talk of county libraries, but little understanding even among professional library workers of precisely what the county system proposes to accomplish and how it functions. Virtually nothing of value has been written about county libraries; no serious effort has been made to bring the idea to library trustees and the community leaders in states where it could be applied with very great advantage. I would suggest, therefore, that the Corporation could perform a notable service by following a plan something like this: First, cause a careful study to be made of the county library system as it operates in California and Oregon and wherever else anything of importance has been done. A report of semi-popular character which would deserve and secure wide publicity would be of great value. Not only would it popularize the idea but it would be useful in library schools in setting before students the present status of this branch of library service.
>
> Having made such a study and report, the Corporation might well follow it up by fostering demonstration units. The idea is to select typical counties which already have a successful county system and make of them models, experimental plants, for the sole purpose of promoting county library work throughout the country. . . .
>
> Such model units would serve a very useful function in providing suitable places for observation and practice for those students in library schools taking special training for service in

Preparation of the Report

> county systems. Indeed this function alone would justify the expenditure necessary to establish one or more units within reach of library schools which are called upon to train for county library service. It is my opinion that money and effort put into some plan of this kind would be more fruitful in promoting library service in small towns and rural communities than larger amounts spent in establishing additional library schools.[76]

In offering an interim proposal for action until county library service could be organized effectively, Williamson again revealed his reliance on a certification program by which levels of service would be defined. He proposed that, while awaiting the development of the county library system, libraries secure librarians with college education and professional training when economically possible, but if that were not possible, to

> secure as librarian a person with high school education, give her the technical training necessary and a certificate of the clerical, subprofessional class.[77] (Italics mine).

The terminology used was definitely related to the plan of certification advanced in the report of the A. L. A. Committee on National Certification of 1921.

General Criticisms of Existing Library Schools

Having viewed the existing schools, Williamson informed the Corporation that

> the primary need of every library school is better financial support. It is futile to call for higher standards and an extension of facilities until it is possible to pay salaries that will permit of larger staffs and a higher grade of instruction.[78]

The published report, from which the preceding observation and specific recommendations for improving the situation were deleted, bore the overtones of a dirge, for, unrelieved as was the original report of its positive recommendations, it offered only a discomforting estimation of the poverty of the schools, of the teaching staff, and of the equipment. Stating that the staff problem was due to "economic necessities and inadequate standards," Williamson warned that

> tho an increase in salaries will not of itself bring relief, other measures are likely to be of no avail so long as salaries remain at anything like the present level.[79]

In a somewhat compensatory tone, Williamson added later:

> It is fortunate, however, that the schools do take themselves with the utmost seriousness, and by dint of patient and devoted, if not brilliant, effort do achieve results which are surprisingly large when measured by their resources in personnel and equipment.[80]

The curriculum. -- Williamson's conclusion in regard to curriculum content was that "as it now stands [it] represents in the main the current demands of the librarians who employ the graduates and the experience of the graduates themselves,"[81] and he proposed instead that a scientific analysis be made of what training for professional library work should be, and that a curriculum be built upon the results of that analysis. Williamson's own analysis of the existing curricula produced evidence of total disagreement among the schools as to the relative importance of the various subjects, for example, in cataloging in which one school offered 105 hours and another, 35 hours.[82] He noted the lack of emphasis on instruction in the "literature of scientific, technical, business, social, economic, and political subjects in general," and he concluded that neither through the curriculum nor the personnel of the existing schools would trained leadership then demanded be forthcoming.[83]

Preparation of the Report   89

He further advised the Corporation that

> if it is to take an interest in promoting training
> for library work, it should see to it that men
> and women of energy and initiative are brought
> into the schools. 84

<u>Length of the training period and curriculum content.</u> -- Williamson specifically recommended that the first year of training should include content, general and basic, and that in the second year specialized training should be offered. He advised further that students should work for at least one year before returning for the specialized curriculum to be offered in the second year. 85 In making the recommendation Williamson was not making a revolutionary proposal; rather he was agreeing with prevalent ideas, for he wrote:

> The opinion of experienced library workers is
> very decidedly against the two-year general
> course. It is believed that it would be much
> better for the two-year schools to give in one
> year all the essentials of a general professional
> course and then offer a second year of specialized,
> advanced work. 86

The opinion was reinforced by the failure of two-year graduates to show marked superiority over the one-year graduates and, even more practically, by the minimal differential in salary between the two groups.

<u>Specialized study in the second year.</u> -- Williamson envisioned the specialized programs as being offered in different schools, for example, children's work at Western Reserve University, and usually for small groups of students. His plan emerged as follows:

> The number of students enrolling for this type
> of specialized training would not usually be large
> enough to require formal lecture courses by the
> library school faculty. The instruction in library
> subjects would therefore be given largely by read-

ings, problems, discussions, and individual conferences with the instructors in charge. Instruction in related subjects would ordinarily be given through the regular courses in cooperating institutions. Field work should occupy a large part of the student's time and be very carefully planned and supervised by practical experts in the special field. . . . In a course of this kind, the acquisition of skill is a definite objective. [87]

He identified the group for which specialized training should be provided at once as high school librarians for whom the following elements were cited for inclusion in a second year program: "(1) special study of high school library problems, supplementing and adapting the general course; (2) special study and training in educational subjects: history of education, educational psychology, and the high school curriculum; (3) extensive field practice."[88]

Williamson was less detailed in his survey of the needs of other specialized groups, particularly those interested in college and university librarianship. He deplored the inadequacies of the faculties and, instead of offering a positive program, he quoted a university librarian who maintained that

'The best reference people I have met in my own experience are not library school graduates but university-trained people who have somehow gone into library work. . . . I would rather have such people with an imperfect knowledge of library technique, than the best trained technician who lacks university training and some graduate study.'[89]

Other areas referred to as requiring specialized study were: (1) cataloguing and classification; (2) library administration; (3) county and rural library service; (4) the business library; (5) teaching in library schools. The report cannot be criticized, however, for its failure to discuss

Preparation of the Report   91

each suggested specialization since Williamson stated that his purpose was "merely to suggest in broad outline some of the types of specialized curricula."[90]

Methods of instruction.[91] -- Though Williamson commented on the excessive dependence of the schools on the lecture method he acknowledged that the school authorities recognized its limitation. He scored the part-time system of instruction as further evidence of the attempt to conduct a school on too limited a budget and he attributed some of the ineffectual teaching to the absence of suitable text-books.[92]

Williamson re-evaluated the program of "field work"[93] and concluded that the program was generally unsatisfactory. He proposed instead a carefully prepared program of observation and inspection trips. He advised the schools that they

> should be quite frank to admit that they cannot turn out skilled workers, and merely attempt to give instruction which can be relied upon to make the acquisition of skill speedy and certain. With this clear understanding, the schools may properly continue to include in their one-year, general course a small amount of so-called practical work, solely as a means of increasing the efficiency of classroom instruction, and not at all with an idea of producing skilled library workers.[94]

Entrance requirements. -- In reviewing the admission requirements which, except in the New York State Library School and at Illinois, consisted only of entrance examinations, Williamson commented on their crude and unscientific composition and their inadequacy in testing the candidate's general education and information. He concluded:

> As an educational preparation for library work nothing has been discovered which can take the place of a thorough college course of varied content.[95]

As a solution to the problem, Williamson suggested the possibility of a uniform examination but admitted that there seemed to be little likelihood of the adoption of such a plan. He questioned also the reliability of the personality test and the interviews required by many of the schools since "the impressionistic method of the interview seems likely to reflect the personality of the interviewer as much as that of the interviewed."96

Williamson particularly questioned the requirements of previous experience in library work, the acquiring of library handwriting, and the use of the typewriter. He was so convinced that the basic entrance requirement should be educational that he stated:

> The fundamental viewpoint of this report is that professional library work requires a college education or its full equivalent. 97

Location of the library school. -- Williamson stated firmly as another fundamental concept of his study that the library school should be organized as a department of a university rather than in a public, state, or municipal library. 98

Recruiting for library work. -- In viewing the recruiting program, Williamson commented on the ineffectual efforts of library schools and of the practicing librarians, and on the low esteem in which library work was held both because of its clerical operations and its being considered "women's work." 99

As incentives to a more profitable recruiting program, Williamson suggested internal improvements: that the schools be elevated to graduate status by improving staff qualifications, curriculum content, and methods of teaching. Once again he adjudged the proper place for the school as the university, relegating to public libraries the training of recruits for the sub-professional grades. William-

Preparation of the Report 93

son predicted that

> when professional education of librarians has gone where all other professional education is going--to the university--a long step will have been taken toward a solution of the recruiting problem. 100

He was equally aware that the schools within the university atmosphere would need financial assistance to offer students, for he wrote:

> Library schools connected with the universities especially feel the need of scholarships and fellowships to enable them to compete with graduate schools which draw some of the best students into teaching and other lines of work by offering inducements of this kind. 101

He was even more firmly insistent that a distinction be made between professional library work and that type of work dependent on the "skillful use of hands in the mechanical operations" of the library before it could appeal, even with fellowships and scholarships, to the better type of college men and women. 102 Having estimated the need of the schools, he proposed that the Corporation, in order to aid in the recruiting of promising college graduates, both men and women, establish a few fellowships to be awarded on a competitive basis. 103

Summary. -- Williamson's recommendations for the improvement of library training may be summarized as follows: (1) education for librarianship should consist of one year of general professional instruction offered to college graduates [or to those possessing an education fully equivalent to that of the college graduate]; (2) library schools should be associated with universities, not with publicly supported institutions such as public libraries; (3) the second year of training should be a year of specialization; (4) schools should develop special areas of specialization, for example, the University of California should specialize in county library work; (5) students, before entering the specialized programs, should have had some practical experience after completing the first year of general professional training; (6) correspondence courses should be incorporated into the curriculum, especially at the school to be established at Columbia University; (7) library schools should not expect to produce skilled professional librarians.

It was with the intent of those recommendations that Williamson viewed specifically the schools which were receiving or were asking to receive Carnegie funds. His conclusions in regard to those schools reflected particularly two of his concepts: (1) that a college degree should be a prerequisite for admission; (2) that the schools should be associated with universities. In the following chapter a survey of the recommendations made to the Carnegie Corporation will be outlined.

Notes

1.   Letter from C. C. Williamson, January 3, 1920, p. 2. (in the files of Williamson.)

2.   Ibid., p. 1. Those were indeed high words of praise for the New York State Library School. Williamson referred favorably again to the School in the published report, Training for Library Service, when, in noting that 60 per cent of all the men trained for library work had studied at the New York State Library School, he concluded: "If we are to judge by the statistics, college men prefer a school of the highest standards which comes most nearly to meeting the requirements of a professional school organized on a graduate basis." Williamson II, p. 77.

3.   Ibid.

4.   Ibid.

Preparation of the Report								95

5. Charles Clarence Williamson, Andrew Carnegie: His Contribution to the Public Library Movement; a Commemorative Address; Founder's Day Address delivered at the Library School, Western Reserve University, Cleveland, June 15th, 1920 (Cleveland: Western Reserve University, 1920), p. 13.

6. For his earlier ideas, see the discussion of the content of his article, "The Need of a Plan for Library Development," p. 27-32 of this book.

7. Williamson, Andrew Carnegie, p. 14.

8. Publicly is emphasized since it is known that Alvin S. Johnson had made similar statements in his report which was made available only to a few. In his report, Johnson had said: "Philanthropic funds might with propriety be diverted from the provision of buildings to the improvement of facilities for training, if the object in view is the maximum development of effective library service. It is worth noting that at an earlier point in the American library movement, when the emphasis rested more heavily than at present upon the need for buildings, Mr. Carnegie made liberal donations to the cause of library training." Johnson, op. cit., p. 18.

9. Williamson, Andrew Carnegie, p. 4.

10. Ibid., p. 10.

11. Ibid.

12. Ibid., p. 12.

13. Ibid., p. 7.

14. Ibid.

15. Ibid., p. 13.

16. Letter from Andrew Carnegie, May 15, 1890, quoted in Grosvenor Dawe, Melvil Dewey, Seer: Inspirer: Doer, 1851-1931: Biographic Compilation ("Library Edition," Lake Placid Club, Essex Co., N.Y.: Melvil Dewey Biography, 1932), p. 200.

17. Ibid., p. 14.

18.   Williamson, "Summary of Report," p. 2.

19.   Ibid.

20.   Ibid.

21.   Thirty-five years after Williamson delivered the address at Western Reserve University, he recalled that in his speech on Andrew Carnegie he had "avoided spelling out the fact that support of library schools was not a part of the approved program of the Carnegie Corporation--not yet certainly. That was not the time or place to dash the hopes that were running high." Letter from C. C. Williamson, May 23, 1955. (in the files of Vann.) Williamson's recollection of the speech is at variance with its actual content, for though he did avoid spelling out the fact, he was not reluctant to make a public statement that the Carnegie Corporation had done more to promote free libraries through assisting the four library schools which were or had received Carnegie funds than through any like expenditure.

22.   American Library Association, "Report of Committee on Nominations," A. L. A. Bulletin, XIII (May, 1919), 91.

23.   C. C. Williamson, "A Look Ahead for the Small Library," A. L. A. Bulletin, XIII (July, 1919), 141-146.

24.   C. C. Williamson, "Some Present-Day Aspects of Library Training," A. L. A. Bulletin (July, 1919), 120-126.

25.   Williamson, "A Look Ahead," p. 141.

26.   Ibid.

27.   Ibid., p. 144.

28.   Ibid.

29.   Williamson II, p. 133.

30.   Williamson, "Some Present-Day Aspects," p. 121.

31.   Williamson I, p. 176.

32.   "Committee of Five: On a Library Survey," A. L. A. Bulletin, XIII (March, 1919), 32. The other committee members were: Arthur E. Bostwick, chairman, Linda A.

Eastman, Carl H. Milam, and Azariah S. Root. Since the
name of Williamson is appended to the report presented at
the Asbury Park Conference, it seems safe to assume that
he accepted the appointment and expressed some opinions on
the subject to the chairman. American Library Association,
Committee of Five on Library Service, "Report, 1919,"
A. L. A. Bulletin, XIII (July, 1919), 326-328.

33. American Library Association, Committee of Five on
Library Service, "Report, 1919," p. 327.

34. American Library Association, Special A. L. A. Committee on Certification, Standardization, and Library Training, "Report, 1920," quoted in full in Williamson I, Appendix V, p. 253.

35. American Library Association, Committee on National
Certification, "Report, 1921," quoted in Williamson I, Appendix VI, p. 255-276.

36. Other evidences of his absorption were his speeches
made on "Personnel Specifications for Library Work" and his
presidential address made at the New York Library Association. It was in the latter speech that he recognized the
spirit of discontent among non-school librarians who were
offering opposition to a program of certification through an
organization composed largely of non-school people, the
Library Workers Association. Not only did he reprimand
the Library Workers Association for its attitude, he referred
to it again in both the published and unpublished reports on
library training. C. C. Williamson, "Personnel Specifications for Library Work: a Project," PL, XXVI (June, 1921),
297-301. New York Library Association, "'Library Week'
at Cornell University," LJ, XLVI (October 15, 1921), 856-864. Williamson I, p. 146; Williamson II, p. 105.

37. American Library Association, Committee on National
Certification, "Report, 1921," p. 263.

38. Williamson probably prepared the Committee report
while completing his inspection tour of the library schools,
for on May 2, 1921, he forwarded to his Committee members a draft of the report to be presented at Swampscott.
The draft, written by Williamson, represented the interpretation of the views of the individual members of the Committee. Letter from C. C. Williamson, May 2, 1921.

39.   American Library Association, "Proceedings, 1921," A. L. A. Bulletin, XV (May, 1921), 168.

40.   "Midsummer [i. e. Midwinter] Meetings, A. L. A. Council," LJ, XLVI (December 15, 1921), 1035-1036.

41.   "Chicago Mid-Winter Meetings," A. L. A. Bulletin, XVI (January, 1922), 13.

42.   Williamson I, p. 5.

43.   Williamson, "Notes," p. 6-7.

44.   "New York State Library School," PL, XXVI (January, 1921), 48.

45.   "Simmons College," PL, XXVI (February, 1921), 104.

46.   "St. Louis [Library School]", PL, XXVI (February, 1921), 104.

47.   "Carnegie Library, Atlanta," PL, XXVI (July, 1921), 435.

48.   It has been possible to identify the schools represented by code numbers in the statistical tables found on p. 22, 35, [72], and 73 of the published report by comparing the table, "Salaries of the Directors, Principals, and Leading Instructors of Library Schools," in the original report which contains the names of the schools (p. 102) with that same table in the published report wherein the code numbers have been substituted for the names. (p. 73).
Williamson believed that the key had been lost because of the destruction of much of the documentary material relating to the study; therefore only the fortuitous retention of the names in the original report has made it possible to identify the schools.

49.   Williamson I, p. 8.

50.   Williamson I, p. 41; Williamson II, p. 25.

51.   "Williamson, Charles Clarence," LJ, XLVI (May 15, 1921), 478.

52.   Williamson I, p. 178. The italicized statement was omitted from the published report of 1923.

Preparation of the Report

53. In a letter to William Warner Bishop, Williamson stated that the Carnegie report had been submitted to the Corporation the first of December. Letter from C. C. Williamson, February 25, 1922.

54. Letter from Herbert Putnam to the Carnegie Corporation In Re: Survey by Dr. C. C. Williamson of Training for Library Work, March 23, 1922. (in the files of C. C. Williamson).

55. Ibid., p. 1-2.

56. Ibid., p. 2.

57. Letter from Herbert Putnam, March 30, 1922. (in the files of C. C. Williamson).

58. Carnegie Corporation of New York, Memorandum, "Appendix F," p. 2.

59. Williamson I, p. 11; Williamson II, p. 4.

60. Williamson I, p. 169; Williamson II, p. 121.

61. Williamson I, p. 180; Williamson II, p. 129.

62. Ibid.; Ibid.

63. Williamson, "Summary of Report," p. 9.

64. Ibid. William Warner Bishop later criticized the report of 1923, which he had read in galley proof, for its emphasis on certification. He wrote: "I am not certain, either, of the wisdom of building so much of your argument about your plan of certification. As you know, I am heartily in accord with that plan, and it is not because I do not believe in it that I question the wisdom of making it such a prominent part of the Report. After all, a report by an expert is not strengthened by too much dwelling upon a single remedial measure." Letter from William W. Bishop, April 3, 1923. (in the files of C. C. Williamson).

65. Williamson, "Summary of Report," p. 10.

66. Williamson I, p. 160; Williamson II, p. 115. Omitted from the published report is the last half of the sentence, "nor are they in general inclined to experiment with new ideas."

67. Williamson I, p. 165; Williamson II, p. 119.

68. Ibid., p. 166; Ibid.

69. Williamson was to see his proposal for correspondence instruction implemented at the School of Library Service which was established at Columbia University with Williamson as Director, for the American Correspondence School of Librarianship was "transferred with all its assets, good will and students in good standing to Columbia University to be administered jointly by the School of Library Service and the Home Study Department." "In the Library World. New York," LJ, LIII (April 1, 1928), 318. The American Correspondence School of Librarianship had been established in 1923, under the auspices of H. P. Gaylord; Forrest B. Spaulding served as business director, Azariah Smith Root, former chairman of the Committee on Library Training and president of the American Library Association in 1921-1922, director. Williamson I, p. 167.

70. Ibid., p. 72; Williamson II, p. 49. The published report did not indicate in any way that Williamson had made a recommendation to the Corporation. It simply referred to the need of text-books for correspondence courses.

71. Williamson I, p. 74.

72. Ibid., p. 198.

73. Williamson I, p. 184; Williamson II, p. 133.

74. Ibid., p. 185. That particular sentence has been omitted from the published report.

75. Williamson II, p. 100.

76. Williamson I, p. 205-206.

77. Ibid., p. 186; Williamson II, p. 135. In both reports he further identified the sub-professional class as "the lowest standard recognized in the certification system."

78. Williamson I, p. 223. Note similarity of this statement to that made in the letter to William F. Yust on January 3, 1920.

79. Williamson I, p. 58; Williamson II, p. 38.

Preparation of the Report 101

80. Ibid., p. 63; Ibid., p. 42.

81. Ibid., p. 40; Ibid., p. 24.

82. Ibid., p. 30; Ibid., p. 22.

83. Ibid., p. 41; Ibid., p. 25.

84. Ibid., p. 40.

85. Ibid., p. 127-142; Ibid., p. 91-102.

86. Ibid., p. 130; Ibid., p. 93.

87. Ibid., p. 140-141; Ibid., p. 101.

88. Ibid., p. 131-132; Ibid., p. 94.

89. Ibid., p. 132; Ibid., p. 95.

90. Ibid., p. 134; Ibid., p. 96.

91. Ibid., p. 60-69; Ibid., p. 40-47.

92. An entire chapter was devoted to textbooks. Williamson I, p. 70-75, Williamson II, p. 48-52. Omitted from the published report, however, was the specific recommendation that the Corporation offer financial assistance in the preparation of text-books. Williamson I, p. 74.

93. Ibid., p. 76-95; Ibid., p. 53-68.

94. Ibid., p. 91; Ibid., p. 64. Wording changes slightly in published report; "The schools should not hesitate to admit . . . "

95. Ibid., p. 45; Ibid., p. 28.

96. Ibid., p. 49; Ibid., p. 31.

97. Ibid., p. 97; Ibid., p. 70. Wording changed in the published report to read: "One of the fundamental viewpoints of this report . . ."

98. Ibid., p. 121-126; Ibid., p. 86-90.

99. Ibid., p. 149; Ibid., p. 107.

100. Ibid., p. 151; Ibid., p. 109.
101. Ibid., p. 152; Ibid.
102. Ibid., p. 149; Ibid., p. 107.
103. Ibid., p. 153.

Chapter 4

In Fulfillment of Objective One

In fulfillment of objective one of the study, to aid the Corporation "specifically in respect to existing subsidies and pending requests for aid in establishing other schools," Williamson examined critically those schools which had received, were receiving, or were wanting to receive Carnegie funds and made certain recommendations concerning those schools. His report on those schools and the recommendations will be presented in this chapter as follows: (1) the library school situation in New York City; (2) the New England situation; (3) Pennsylvania's needs; (4) Western Reserve University Library School; (5) the Library School of the Carnegie Library of Atlanta; (6) library schools of the West Coast.

The Library School Situation in New York City

Williamson was well aware of the Corporation's concern over the New York Public Library School, for not only was the origin of the study traceable to the resolution accompanying the appropriation for the School for 1918, Williamson had devoted in his "Notes on the Aims" a special section to "The Problem in New York City."[1] In it he identified the problem as being the most complicated and important, noting that despite the demand for library workers in the city and its adjacent areas, training facilities were neither organized nor directed toward meeting the need.

Williamson felt, however, that "by proper centralization of effort, by making use of the unequalled facilities for 'laboratory' work and study in allied fields" an institution could be organized which might not only remedy the local situation but might also provide two, of many, things for which there was a nation-wide need:

> (a) Facilities for training those who are to give instruction in library work; and
>
> (b) Advanced and specialized study of a character needed in important lines of library work and nowhere available at the present time. [2]

It is not surprising to find Williamson reiterating this opinion when, in regard to the New York Public Library School, he raised the question as to whether the time had not come

> to effect a reorganization which will enable it to take full advantage of the unique opportunity presented to a professional library school in New York City. [3]

While raising the question of reorganization he praised the School highly in comparing it to other schools:

> In every respect this school has made a creditable record as measured by the work of the best of the other library schools. It has been economically and efficiently administered, relatively high standards of instruction have been maintained, and the graduates have done well in comparison with those of other schools. [4]

Nevertheless Williamson was content neither with the location of the School nor with its curriculum.

Citing the New York Public Library School's lack of a connection with an educational institution, Williamson suggested that the School become affiliated with Columbia University in some way as had Teachers' College, or that it be organized within the University as had the School of Business and Journalism.[5] He readily admitted that the suggestion for affiliation was not completely new, and referred to an earlier proposal for the establishment of a graduate school of library administration at Columbia. This proposal was disapproved by Williamson because (1) the plan ignored the existence of the New York Public Library School; (2) the costly scheme called for an annual income of $108,000 and a building of $500,000; (3) the program did not contemplate correspondence or other methods of instruction; (4) the proposed two-year course of study emphasized general training with little opportunity for specialization.[6]

The benefits resulting from the establishment of a strong professional school in New York were enumerated as (1) stimulating the development of other library schools on a proper professional basis, inducing weaker schools to drop back to their proper status as training classes, and discouraging the tendency in public and university libraries to start library schools without adequate personnel and financial resources;[7] (2) development of specialized training; (3) development of training courses for teachers; (4) development of short, intensive courses, and perhaps winter courses, for which credit toward the professional degree could be given; (5) development of correspondence study.[8]

The curriculum. -- In contrast to the curriculum of existing schools, which represented, as earlier noted, content requirements as demanded by librarians who were employing the graduates and by the experience of the graduates themselves,[9] Williamson felt that the proposed school
> should not confine itself merely to acquainting students with existing knowledge and practice. As a part of its advanced or specialized work leading to the master's degree, it should be constantly conducting surveys and original investigations.[10]

To provide subjects for investigation, Williamson proposed that a "library information service" be conducted under the auspices of the school.

Exhibit of library equipment. -- A final suggestion, reminiscent of Melvil Dewey's earlier scheme, was the suggestion that the school

> should organize and keep up to date a permanent exhibit of library equipment and methods, to be used primarily for teaching purposes but freely available also to anyone interested. Model book collections for different purposes might be included in the permanent exhibit. Traveling exhibits of various kinds might be prepared for sending out to other library schools, training classes, etc. [11]

Recommendation to the Corporation. -- In asking the Trustees to consider the establishment of a school at Columbia University, Williamson advised:

> If the Carnegie Corporation is prepared to assist in any way in promoting training for library work, it is the writer's opinion that it would be better to develop one strong school than to continue indefinitely to grant small subsidies to many. Besides the schools already subsidized or supported by the Corporation, there are several others whose work would be materially improved by a comparatively small amount of financial assistance, but it is believed that library training and the development of library service in general would benefit more from the existence of one school located in New York City with sufficient resources to set standards which other schools would have to approximate or disappear. [12]

The New England Situation

On the assumption that in any well conceived plan for the organization of professional library training in the United States a library school should be located in or near Boston, Williamson examined the Simmons College School of Library

Science because, as he reported, "it was learned that some special reference . . . might be in order."[13]

Williamson found that the unique situation at Simmons reflected the plan of the School which had been organized in 1902 as a vocational college for women and was composed of eight departments of which library science was one. Within the School of Library Science two programs were being conducted: one, a four-year course, in each year of which an increasing amount of vocational training was included; the other, a one-year course for women graduates of other colleges and for those who had acquired three years of academic study elsewhere. For each program the degree of Bachelor of Science was awarded.

After surveying the program and granting that it may or may not be better than that of other schools, Williamson questioned the advisability of both general college courses and vocational courses:

> . . . in my judgment the professional librarian should have had a well-rounded four-year college course before taking the vocational study.[14]

He added, however,

> if it is necessary for the librarian to get along with less than a full college course, I would prefer to have him complete three years of liberal studies entirely outside the vocational atmosphere.[15]

Granting for the moment that the Simmons graduate was better equipped than the high school graduate who had completed a one-year library school course, Williamson nevertheless anticipated that, when other library schools were placed on a graduate basis, the Simmons graduate would then have inferior training. He warned that unless it gave up its four-year program and confined its library school to a one-year program, Simmons could not reach the standards of the best library schools. While praising the School for its strong faculty and the advantages of its location in Boston, Williamson noted (1) the inadequate library facilities of the college and questioned if the students derived benefit from the libraries in Boston; (2) the need of a connection with a university "most likely to insist on the highest standards and able to offer library school students instruction in a wide range of subjects to fit for specialized library service";[16] (3) the exclusion of men from the School. On the third point Williamson stated emphatically that

> the one strong library school in the New England states should not only be open to men, but should be of such a character that it would attract able men into the library profession.[17]

No recommendation. -- While insisting that it was far from his thoughts to suggest that Simmons College should not have a library school, Williamson advised the Carnegie Corporation that if it should

> undertake to promote professional library training it should throw its support to institutions which in respect to their location, organization, and general relations naturally have a place in a well planned program. Consideration should also be given to the need of checking the feminization of library work as a profession.[18]

The implication is clear that Williamson made no specific recommendation that the Corporation assist the School either in its present or future program.

Comment in the published report. -- In the published report Williamson referred to the Simmons plan in the chapter on "Courses, Credit, Degrees, and Status," publicizing thereby his objection to the inclusion of vocational training in an undergraduate program. He advised that

> while comparatively little of the vocational work

> in Simmons is given before the junior year, it
> would seem better to postpone all vocational
> courses until the senior year, and better still,
> until after the bachelor's degree has been received.[19]

Response from Simmons College. -- Had Simmons College known of the confidential report being presented to the Corporation, it could well have anticipated the recommendation. A response to the published criticism was made, however, by June R. Donnelly, director of Simmons College Library School:

> That is a point on which we retain an open mind,
> as we have to reconsider it every year. I should
> have been glad for new evidence. So far the
> school has not recommended the change because
> its faculty is not persuaded the other methods
> [sic] is not better for the students. . . . We
> are tempted often, financially, to change the
> policy. It would be cheaper and easier to administer the school on Dr. Williamson's plan.[20]

Pennsylvania's Needs

Though there had been two library schools in the state of Pennsylvania until 1914--Drexel Institute Library School in Philadelphia and the Carnegie Library School in Pittsburgh--only the Pittsburgh school was functioning after 1914. The need of even one library school was questioned by Williamson who, commenting that librarians in eastern Pennsylvania felt that the school in Pittsburgh meant nothing to them, stated

> There may actually be some question as to
> whether even one high grade library school is
> needed in Pennsylvania at the present time.
> Certainly there is no need for two.[21]

Drexel Institute Library School. -- Such a feeling in the eastern part of the state could have been expected because of the efforts to revive the Drexel Institute Library School, a revival urged by the Alumnae Association. It had in 1921 appointed a committee, consisting of Grace D. Rose, Sarah C. N. Bogle, former principal of the Carnegie Library School of Pittsburgh, and Caroline F. Webster, "to communicate with the committee of the A. L. A. on training and with the Carnegie Corporation on professional training to ascertain the need for more library schools."[22]

No reference was made to the accomplishments of the Alumnae Committee but it can be assumed that the Corporation, if guided by the Williamson recommendations, would have been unresponsive to the plans for re-opening the School. In spite of this, however, the School was reopened[23] for the school year beginning September 25, 1922, several months after the formal presentation of the Williamson report to the Corporation. The revival of the School was hastened by the appointment of a new president of the Institute, Dr. K. G. Matheson who, as a former trustee of the Carnegie Library in Atlanta, Georgia, was not unfamiliar with a library school. Evincing his familiarity with the school, he appointed as director of the Drexel School, Ann Wallace Howland, the first director of the Carnegie Library School of Atlanta.[24]

It is possible that Williamson would have been more emphatic in his objection to the School had he anticipated the appointment of Mrs. Howland because of his dissatisfaction with the Carnegie School of Atlanta, the development of which had been patterned by the director before her marriage.

Though the Williamson report contained no reference to the agitation for the re-opening of the School, a footnote was added to the published report to the effect that

Since this report was completed the Drexel Institute Library School has been revived by the new President of the Institute, Dr. K. G. Matheson.[25] The published report retained the information relating to the discontinuance of the School, the reasons being given as (1) demand for its graduates too slight; (2) salaries for graduates too small to justify any further expenditure; (3) per capita cost of maintaining the Library School higher than any other department in the Institute; (4) though designed primarily as a school for Philadelphia, only seven graduates in five years were taken directly into the general libraries of Philadelphia.[26]

One might interpret Williamson's following comment on the discontinuance of the School as indicative of his concern over Drexel and the similarities of library school problems:

> The considerations which led to giving up the Drexel Institute Library School might almost equally well be used to urge the discontinuance of all library schools. Enrolment everywhere is small, per capita cost of training high, and salaries paid to graduates are uniformly lower than in any other field of work. No one, however, who has the slightest appreciation of the importance of trained library service would suggest giving up all the schools. On the contrary, the situation points to the opposite conclusion. The schools should be strengthened in every way, enrolment multiplied, standards of fitness for library work raised, and salaries increased to a point that will lead college men and women to look upon library work as a desirable career.[27]

The preceding paragraph was not deleted from the published report; significantly deleted, however, was Williamson's own evaluative statement previously quoted in which he questioned the need of even one high grade library school in Pennsylvania.

Carnegie Library School of Pittsburgh

Williamson's questioning of the necessity for even one high grade library school in Pennsylvania focused attention on the Carnegie Library School of Pittsburgh, which he admitted offered a more difficult problem than did Western Reserve University Library School. The problem related to the desirability of developing the general course, added to the curriculum in 1919, "to a point where this school will rank with the other one-year professional schools."[28] It had become intensified by the fact that the School, originally a School for Training Children's Librarians, had in 1918 added a specialized course in school library work and in 1919, a general course, with the result that the School was "attempting to combine general and specialized instruction within the one-year course."[29] Even with these changes, it was still being recognized as a special school for training children's librarians.

In appraising the curriculum Williamson could have easily employed the term "core curriculum" as a descriptive phrase, for he summarized it thus:

> In the first semester a group of basic subjects common to the three courses is given to all the students. In the second semester they elect to go on with the general course, to take special training for work with children, or to prepare for school library work.[30]

The difficulties which, according to Williamson, would prevent the School's achieving a proper professional basis were: (1) the relationship of the School with the Carnegie Institute of Technology, with which it had had nominal affiliation since 1916 and which had led to the consequent absence of a university relationship considered necessary for the proper development of a library school; (2) the directorship of the School's being held by the director of the Carnegie

In Fulfillment of Objective One 113

Library of Pittsburgh; (3) the housing of the School in the
Public Library; (4) the lack of interest or voice in the
management of the School both by the faculty and by the
administrative officers of the Institute; (5) the inadequacies
of the city of Pittsburgh in offering a variety of libraries
for laboratory experience;[31] (6) the limitations of the Public
Library itself as a laboratory for field work, except in its
central department, because of weakness of personnel and
backwardness in developing a popular library service; (7)
the direction of the Apprentice Class of the Public Library
by the Library School.[32]

Report on the Carnegie Institute. -- The report on
the Carnegie Library School and its difficulties becomes
more meaningful when read as a supplementary report to
the one made by Williamson, in 1921, as a member of a
specially appointed commission to survey the Carnegie Institute of Pittsburgh for the Carnegie Corporation. Williamson
and J. C. Christensen, assistant treasurer of the University
of Michigan,[33] surveyed the Library and the Library School,
submitting their reports, with those of the other experts, in
less than three weeks.

Williamson reported on both the Library and the
School in all but financial matters. He did note, however,
that the School was as well supported financially as any of the
others. He added that, in fact, most of the schools had
budgets less than half that of Pittsburgh. In spite of that,
Williamson concluded that the "annual subsidy, plus tuition
fees, is far from adequate for a really first class professional
library school."[34]

Though Williamson commented only briefly on the
Library School, indicating that the problem would be dealt
with in another report to the Corporation, his view on the

School in the earlier report was similar to that expressed in the formal report. In attempting to define principles which should guide one's analysis of the problems, he questioned:

> Whether the professional education of librarians should be organized and conducted under the auspices of a library which is a service institution rather than an institution devoted to general and professional education.
>
> Whether the policy of developing a relatively few high-grade, strong professional schools should be preferred to the present practice of multiplying small and comparatively weak schools in many parts of the country. [35]

Though acknowledging that Pittsburgh needed a good training class for clerical and sub-professional assistants, Williamson questioned the need for a professional school in Pittsburgh, particularly if it continued its association with the Carnegie Library of Pittsburgh.

In the Corporation Report, 1921. -- Later, in preparing the formal report on "Training for Library Work," Williamson had crystallized his views on the two questions posed in the "Report of the Survey of Carnegie Institute of Pittsburgh" and was able to propose certain steps which should be taken if an effort were to be made to put the school on a worthy professional basis. Those steps involved: (1) provision of "adequate and suitable quarters outside of the Carnegie Library building; though within easy reach of it";[36] (2) the separation of the directorship of the library and the school with that of the school being given to "an educator of wide experience in professional library work" responsible to the Board of Trustees;[37] (3) the creation by the Trustees of an advisory board, to aid in the conduct of the school, to be composed of the leading library workers and educators of Pennsylvania and perhaps of other states;

In Fulfillment of Objective One   115

(4) the requirement of a college degree as a prerequisite for admission; (5) the offering of one full year of general professional study followed by the specialized work in a second year program [or presumably the elimination of the second semester of specialized work.] Totally lacking was any reference to the School's traditional concern with the training of children's librarians.

<u>Concerning library training for children's librarians.</u> -- Of training for library work with children Williamson had clearly stated:

> Under the plan of organization proposed in this report, specialized training for professional work with children would be given as a second year of library school study, consisting of some technical library courses, with much attention to literature for children, thorough courses in education, child psychology, and the relations of the library to the public school, accompanied by much field work and practice under expert supervision. 38

However, the absence of a positive suggestion that the Carnegie Library School continue to offer or to improve its specialized course in children's work as a second year program was in sharp contrast to the persuasive recommendation that another of the Schools surveyed concentrate on county library work. Since he had referred to the School within the body of the report as follows:

> Specialized curricula have been offered so far by accredited library schools in only two or three instances, the best examples being the courses in children's library work given by the Carnegie Library School of Pittsburgh and Western Reserve University Library School, 39

it may be assumed that he knew of the specialization in the Carnegie Library School. He apparently concluded that Western Reserve University Library School would be better prepared to undertake the program. The assumption seems justified by the following statement from the published report:

> When all professional schools are put on a graduate basis and the work of the first year is organized as a thoroughly well-rounded and complete general course, graduates from all the schools should naturally expect to take a second year of special training wherever accredited courses are offered in the special fields they desire to enter. Graduates from all the schools might go to Western Reserve for children's work.[40]

No recommendation. -- No specific recommendation was made that the Carnegie Library School receive an additional subsidy from the Corporation; nor was it specifically stated that the subsidy it was receiving should cease. It is evident, however, that Williamson was doubtful about the proper course to follow because of the administrative structure subordinating the School to a technological institute and to a public library. His questioning, moreover, of the need for a library school in Pennsylvania would have alone prevented his making a recommendation urging the continuance of the Carnegie Library School of Pittsburgh.

Western Reserve University Library School

Williamson viewed with some misgivings the Library School with which he had at one time been accidentally associated, for after viewing the school's financial status, an income of $6,000, of which two-thirds was used for salaries of the teaching and administrative staff, he concluded:

> In my judgment this school cannot adequately meet the needs of Cleveland and of Ohio for professionally trained librarians on its present income. There is great need for additional instructors and more adequate salaries. Larger

In Fulfillment of Objective One					117

> quarters and better equipment are also a necessity before the school can increase its enrolment and place its instruction on a strictly professional basis.[41]

Noting the pitifully small salary of $1,920 being paid the one full-time instructor, a salary slightly larger than that of the beginning graduate, Williamson praised the staff of the Cleveland Public Library by acknowledging:

> Were it not for the excellent and largely unpaid cooperation of the staff of the Cleveland Public Library this school would find it very difficult to maintain its present standards, which are at present quite as satisfactory as those of other schools--the Pittsburgh School, for example, which has twice as large a budget and fewer students.[42]

Despite the financial impediments, Williamson recognized the initial advantages of the status of the school "as an integral part of a university of proper standing and ideals," of the excellent laboratory facilities offered by the city of Cleveland, of the existence within the Cleveland Public Library of its own training class for clericals and sub-professionals and predicted that "this is one of the library schools which should be able to take the lead in putting its work on a graduate basis".[43]

Not only did Williamson express the hope that the School would put its work on a graduate basis by raising its standards of instruction and its admission requirements to college graduation; he further proposed that

> this or some other school in the Middle West should be in a position to offer a good, intensive short course in the summer for the untrained worker and perhaps also a summer school for library workers with good education who would like to take advantage of an opportunity to get a full library school course and receive the degree by taking courses in the summer.[44]

Though granting the University of Illinois was already offering two summer school programs, Williamson insisted that there should be in Ohio a school prepared to offer such training and he predicted that if Western Reserve University Library School

> does not shortly offer some such form of training in service, the State University or some other institution is likely to do so, with the unhappy result of adding another weak, struggling library school to those already in existence. 45

Recommendation. -- Because of his own strong conviction that the Western Reserve University Library School possessed the potential for becoming a graduate school and because of the need in Cleveland for a graduate professional school of the highest standards, Williamson advised the Corporation that "provided proper development can be assured thereby, money put into an increased endowment for this school would do much to promote and improve library services generally."46

The Library School of the Carnegie Library of Atlanta

The Corporation had been disturbed for some time over the situation in the southern library school which from 1902 to 1920 received a total of $70,500 from Andrew Carnegie and the Corporation. The question being probed was

> whether money given to this school is producing an adequate return in training for librarianship and particularly whether it is filling the needs of the South for trained workers. 47

In seeking an answer to the question, Williamson surveyed the library situation and produced the alarming information that in Georgia, of the thirty libraries supported in whole or in part by public funds, only thirteen had a total income of $1,000 or more. In addition he reported

In Fulfillment of Objective One   119

that 103 counties lacked any kind of library service, and,
most significantly, that

> although the Carnegie Library School of Atlanta
> had been in operation for sixteen years, not a
> single graduate of the school is employed in any
> public library in Georgia, outside of the two
> largest cities--Atlanta and Savannah. 48

From those dismal facts, plus the information that
each of the southeastern states in 1921 furnished, on an
average, only one student each to the School, Williamson
concluded that "the effect of the Atlanta library school on
the library situation in the South is seen to be almost
negligible. "49

Despite that minimal effect, Williamson tended to
favor the retention of a School in Atlanta because of its
central location in Georgia, of the Carnegie Library's status
as the largest and best organized library south of Washington and east of the Mississippi. He noted also the development of library facilities of different types, such as those
to be found at Emory University, Agnes Scott College, and
the University of Georgia. As an additional evidence of the
need for the School, Williamson observed that

> Young women in the South, it is believed, will
> not readily go into library work unless they can
> get their training in the South. 50

His second assumption, concerning the need for the
School, was that

> It is not possible for the South to draw its library workers from the North. Salaries are
> now, and long will be, too low to make that
> possible and the South is convinced that workers
> from the North could not succeed because they
> would fail to understand the situation. 51

Had the South been able to attract northern graduates, the
northern and western library schools were not training for

service in libraries of the kind which prevailed throughout the South;[52] consequently their presence would have alleviated only in part the situation described by Williamson.

Criticisms of the School. -- Williamson compared library development in the South with that in northern and western states at the turn of the century when those states were establishing library commissions to conduct summer schools and other methods of training in service. He noted, however, that the Atlanta School was not attempting to provide such services but was attempting to be a professional school, to use the same methods and to maintain nominally the same standards as the professional schools elsewhere. Of the situation Williamson said:

> I venture to express the opinion that the Atlanta School from the beginning has been guided too closely by the methods and standards of older library schools, instead of studying the needs of the South and then organizing to meet those specific needs. [53]

He further charged that by its efforts to retain membership in the Association of American Library Schools, the School had missed its opportunities of serving small libraries

> which cannot derive much benefit from a school offering only a one-year professional course and maintaining a standard of admission which, though not high, is still high enough to keep out most or all of those who have charge of the public libraries in the smaller cities of the South. [54]

The charge seems somewhat excessive since the Association of American Library Schools was not organized formally until 1915. The major charge could well have been against the imitative zeal of the school from the time of its establishment which prevented its recognition that the South cannot at present supply the students for, or use the graduates of, a professional library school of the standards demanded in other parts of the country. [55]

While urging that the School disregard the standards of the Association "and adopt a course which is likely to be interpreted as evidence of weakness and to result in loss of prestige,"[56] Williamson coldly judged that the School at best

> can only formally comply with the requirements of the Association of American Library Schools. It has not the laboratory facilities, the instructional staff or the student body to compete with the larger and stronger schools. It would not be advisable for a graduate of a southern college, desiring to enter professional library work, to go to the Atlanta School. [57]

Recommendations to the School. -- Williamson's recommendations to the Atlanta School were, then; (1) to take whatever measures are necessary to reach a much larger number of people who can derive some benefit from its instruction; (2) to leave, for the time being, full professional instruction to other schools; (3) to devote itself to something more like extension instruction. [58]

To accomplish its re-defined purpose, Williamson suggested that the School (1) conduct a first-rate training class for assistants in the Atlanta and other public libraries in the South; (2) offer short intensive courses for untrained librarians in charge of small public libraries. [59]

The content of the training class which the Atlanta School would become would not necessarily have differed from that being offered at the time of the survey, according to Williamson. He suggested reorienting the courses towards giving more time to supervised practice and more attention to the community problems of the South and less time to historical aspects of subjects and advanced techniques. The entrance requirement for the course was to be a diploma from an approved high school instead of entrance examinations; for the short intensive course, for those who could not afford the time to complete the regular course, the admission requirement was to be even less.

In re-emphasizing the need for the short intensive courses, Williamson warned that

> this kind of cooperation is seriously limited or made impossible by the organization and methods of a school trying to keep step with professional library schools in parts of the country which are well supplied with summer schools and training courses in addition to the best of the library schools.[60]

Recommendation to the Corporation. -- Because he felt strongly that the School was functioning ineffectually but at the same time that the South needed well educated southern women who had taken their library training in the North, Williamson suggested:

> It would be better for the South if the Carnegie Corporation, instead of keeping the Library School in Atlanta alive on its present basis, were to pay to the eight students the difference between the cost of going to Atlanta and to a northern school.[61]

He later suggested the awarding of scholarships:

> The Carnegie Corporation might render a very important service by offering to young women in the southern states competitive scholarships in northern schools. Holders of scholarships could be selected so as to rouse more interest in library work among the educated women of the South than the existing school at Atlanta can hope to do.[61]

While admitting that his idea of scholarships might not be practicable, Williamson stated that it emphasized the need for the Corporation to consider carefully the "continued support of the Library School of the Carnegie Library of Atlanta as at present conducted."[63]

In Fulfillment of Objective One   123

Library Schools on the West Coast

Two chapters of the report were devoted to training problems on the West Coast: chapter 21, "The Proposed Library School in the Portland (Oregon) Public Library" and chapter 23, "The Riverside Library Service School." The two programs were viewed critically by Williamson because both had been attempting presumably, to secure Carnegie aid in the furtherance of their plans. By a coincidence the removal by death of the dominant personality associated with each of the programs affected to an indeterminate extent the development of library training on the west coast. The following sections summarize the impact of these events on Williamson's decisions after his visit to the Coast.

The Proposed Library School in the
Portland (Oregon) Public Library

Williamson went to Oregon not unfamiliar with the desire of the Library Association of Portland to establish a library school. Not only did he know of the untiring efforts of Mary Frances Isom to secure funds from the Carnegie Corporation before her death in April, 1920,[64] he had considered her as one of the six members of the committee which he would have recommended to undertake a study on library training.[65] Further, he had talked with her about the proposed school and with at least one member of the Board of Trustees and had referred to her as "the efficient and highly esteemed librarian."[66]

Yet he was disappointed in Portland after his visit. In spite of some wholly favorable conditions, such as ample and satisfactory quarters, a well organized and efficient system of both municipal and county libraries, and a demand

for trained personnel, Williamson informed the Corporation:
> It was my conclusion, after personal investigation and conference with various persons in position to give helpful advice, that it would be unwise for the Corporation to finance or endow a library school in Portland at the present time.67

Among the reasons given for the unfavorable decision were these: (1) lack of strong leadership throughout the Portland library;68 (2) objection to staffing of the school by women because of its tendency to deter men from entering; (3) the violation of the principle of encouraging the establishment of library schools in a university environment; (4) problems of recruiting; (5) recognition that pride would encourage each state, Oregon, for example, to "rely on a weak school in Portland rather than a strong one in Seattle or Berkeley or in any state east of the Pacific Coast";69 (6) recognition that other states could present claims as strong as those of Oregon to the Corporation; (7) the failure of Ethel R. Sawyer to impress Williamson with her fitness to direct a program.

Disapproval of Miss Sawyer. -- While Williamson was impressed favorably by the personality of Joseph F. Daniels of the Riverside Library Service School, he was not similarly impressed by Miss Sawyer who had been designated dean apparent of the Portland school. In wholly uncomplimentary terms Williamson thus appraised Miss Sawyer:
> I cannot believe that she is a proper person to be placed in charge of, or even to teach in, a library school, where orderliness and business methods should constantly be inculcated, not only by precept, but by example, on the part of every officer and instructor with whom the student comes in contact.70

In re-emphasizing his total rejection of the Portland situation, he concluded:

> In my judgment, the library school of which
> Miss Sawyer was made director would inevitably
> be a failure. In my judgment also, a librarian
> and a board of trustees who have in mind a type
> of library school of which she would be a worthy
> head do not have a proper conception of standards
> of professional education. [71]

<u>Recommendation to the Corporation.</u> -- While Williamson emphatically stated that it would be unwise to endow a library school in Portland at the present time, he granted that

> Conditions may change so that at some future
> time a library school could properly be established in Portland, even with financial assistance
> from the Carnegie Corporation. [72]

He added as a precautionary warning, in keeping with his concept that library schools should be affiliated with universities, the following:

> It might be wise, also in aiding any public institution, municipal or state, to establish a
> library school to require the institution to pledge
> a reasonable share of the total budget out of
> total funds. If this were done, public library
> boards would not be so eager to maintain professional schools for the benefit of the country. [73]

<u>The enigma.</u> -- Left unanswered in the Portland situation is the question of what would have happened had Miss Isom lived. Her death occurred in April, 1920, almost a year before Williamson's visit, whereas Daniels' death was to occur after his visit to Riverside. Could she, through the strength of her personality, have influenced Williamson to recommend an endowment? Whatever her virtues, it was she who had placed Miss Sawyer in charge of the training class, a position for which Williamson regarded her as competent only if the training had been planned for clerical workers on the library staff.

The Riverside (California) Library Service School

There were three library schools in California at the time of Williamson's visit: the State University Library School, the Los Angeles Public Library School,[74] and the Riverside Library Service School. It was to the last mentioned, however, that Williamson gave special attention. He did so because, according to the first paragraph of chapter 23, having inferred that the school had been seeking an endowment from the Corporation, he had conscientiously made an effort to understand the significance of the Riverside School.[75]

It seems equally true that the School dominated his attention because of the sometimes recalcitrant but ever towering personality of Joseph F. Daniels, the director. So powerful indeed was its effect on Williamson that he was willing to make a favorable recommendation after his observation of the School in action. It is possible that, had Daniels lived, the history of library school development on the west coast might have been quite different, but his death on September 16, 1921, which occurred during Williamson's writing of the report, required Williamson to consider training from a more objective viewpoint than had been evidenced earlier. Because of the changes in his thinking and recommendations wrought by Daniels' death, the chapter may be examined as Williamson's ideas <u>before</u> and <u>after</u> that death. Williamson's full recording of the unusual episode has made it possible to view the change in his point of view. He could easily have omitted many of the references which reveal his own vacillations in regard to a policy advocated by himself and also the attitudes of Daniels' associates towards him. Since he preferred to include all the story in the report, a brief review of the details will be given as "Before" and "After."

In Fulfillment of Objective One   127

BEFORE . . .
    The Riverside Library Service School, unorthodox and not a member of the Association of American Library Schools, demonstrated the educational concepts of Joseph F. Daniels and orbited around his personality. So impressed was Williamson by the program that, while his usual policy was recommending grants only to schools affiliated with universities, he recommended a temporary annual subsidy for the School on the condition that Daniels qualify and seek admission to the Association of American Library Schools.[76] In offering the recommendation Williamson acknowledged that he was making an exception to that policy but that he had been

> captivated by his genius and struck with admiration by the large place he had made for himself and his library in the community and in the affection of a host of friends in Riverside.[77]

In thus recommending Daniels, Williamson was helping to perpetuate a situation of which he had been critical in the schools--the domination of each library school by a single personality. In characterizing that situation Williamson reported:

> Most school principals are conscious of exercising control only to the extent required to prevent overlapping of courses and direct conflict as to rules and practices taught in the schools. As a matter of fact, actual control probably goes much further--so far, indeed, that little scope is left for the originality and enthusiasm of the gifted teacher.[78]

Williamson's own estimation of the School reflected the impact of Daniels' personality on him, for he wrote:

> What I saw going on was not much more than apprentice, on a 'learn by doing' method, but yet I left Riverside feeling that a year spent in that environment, no matter what the character

of the formal instruction, would be excellent
preparation for service in small town and rural
libraries. 79

His view was not shared by others; for example, Dr. H. L.
Leupp, librarian of the University of California and his
colleagues

did not consider that the Riverside School has
had a strong staff, nor did they think it gets a
good class of students or does thorough work.
They evidently would not recommend the Riverside School to University graduates or be willing
to accept graduates of the school for their own
staff. 80

Williamson planned that the School take a leading
position in training for county library service, because of
Daniels' ambition to occupy that field. It failed to materialize
when he learned that Daniels and his fellow librarians,
particularly the State Librarian, Milton H. Ferguson, were
divided over the issue of "contract versus direct county
library system." In view of those divisive attitudes, Williamson concluded that

one could hardly look forward to making the
Riverside School an important training center
for the training of county librarians for service
in California. 81

Recommendation to the Corporation. -- Despite the ad-
verse comments, Williamson praised both the personality and
enthusiasm of Daniels which were magnified because they were

combined with the fact that he already had a school
which, thanks to his natural gift for publicity, was
well advertised, and into which he was putting
and would continue to put a large part of his
energy. 82

In addition he recommended a temporary annual subsidy of "$5,000 a year for the next five years. The sub-
sidy was to be made with the understanding that it might be
continued from year to year beyond that period if conditions

warranted it."83

Williamson recognized, however, that it would have been unwise to have suggested a permanent endowment to "the weakest, most unfortunately located and least necessary school in a state, a school highly unpopular with librarians and state officials," or to Daniels, "an insurgent, always spectacular and always flouting every suggestion of professional or educational standards." Williamson also hesitated because of his concern that such an endowment, to forward looking librarians, might appear to express approval of Daniels' attacks on certification and of his disregard of the Association of American Library Schools. 84

AFTER . . .

That the statement of the influence of Daniels' personality on Williamson is not overexaggerated can be seen from his following reappraisal:

> With Mr. Daniels gone I cannot recommend endowment or other financial support. To do so would be quite inconsistent with the tenor of my report. 85

He reinforced his decision by advising that the School should be abandoned and that the library interests of the state should be centered in the two strategically located schools at Los Angeles and at Berkeley.

Recommendation concerning the State University School. -- Having eliminated any further consideration of the Riverside School, Williamson's final recommendation to the Corporation was "to put the state school on its feet first and bring it into cooperative relations with the Los Angeles School."86 The recommendation, made because of the precarious financial condition of the School whose funds had been slashed from the budget, proposed that the Corporation offer $10,000 next year, provided the legislature would appropriate $5,000 and each year increase its share while the share of the Corporation diminishes and then ceases.[87]

Two possible results of such aids were to be, according to Williamson: (1) the stimulus towards developing in other states proper support of a university library school; (2) the ultimate transfer of the Los Angeles Public Library School to the southern branch of the University of California in Los Angeles "if proper support and administration were assured."[88]

Once again Williamson's interest in county library work emerged as he anticipated the development in the School of a training program for county library work which would train leaders for service in several states. He mentioned particularly the state of Oregon which would be better served by a "strong school in Berkeley making a special feature of county work"[89] than by its own weak school. As a unique contribution he urged the judicious expenditure of funds for the establishment of a county library demonstration unit to be used as a laboratory by the University of California Library School.

<u>Summation of advice to the Corporation.</u> -- Williamson emphasized that he was not attempting to outline a plan for organizing and developing library training on the Coast. He was instead making suggestions

> as affording a possible method by which a comparatively small amount of money used to develop a state system will in the end accomplish far more than if put into the Riverside School where it cannot call forth additional state or local support and can only serve to divide or weaken the forces needed for any real improvement of training facilities in the state.[90]

Summary of Recommendations

Williamson's specific recommendations in regard to the schools reflected first his conviction that the library schools should be associated with universities and, secondly, a corollary conviction, that professional library schools should not be affiliated with public institutions. In three instances Williamson recommended that financial assistance be offered and in all three the schools were, or were to be, associated with universities: the school to be established at Columbia University, the Western Reserve University Library School, and the school struggling for recognition at the University of California at Berkeley.

In contrast, his recommendations concerning schools associated with public institutions included no proposals for continuing financial assistance. For the schools receiving Carnegie funds at the time of the study, he recommended: (1) that the New York Public Library School be transferred to Columbia University; (2) that the Library School of the Carnegie Library of Atlanta identify itself as a training school and not attempt to offer professional training. No specific recommendation was made concerning the Carnegie Library School of Pittsburgh. Thus the evaluation of the "Carnegie Schools" by Williamson differed from that of Alvin S. Johnson who earlier had praised the New York Public Library School and the Carnegie Library School of Pittsburgh. He also had omitted any reference to Western Reserve or to the Carnegie Library School of Atlanta.

For the schools not receiving Carnegie funds at the time, but associated with public institutions, Williamson refused to make favorable recommendations. For the two schools which had been seeking Carnegie funds, he made no recommendations, these being the proposed school to be established in Portland, Oregon, and the school already in existence at Riverside California. He recommended instead the abolishment of the latter. In addition, though the Library School of the Los Angeles Public Library presumably had not requested funds, he recommended in the "Summary of Report," its absorption by the School regarded as worthy of aid, the University of California School at Berkeley.

Two additional recommendations made were to prove beneficial, when implemented, to all the schools: (1) that the Corporation subsidize the preparation of textbooks for the improvement of teaching; and (2) that the Corporation offer scholarships and fellowships on a competitive basis to college graduates, both men and women.

Notes

1. Williamson, "Notes," p. 13-14.
2. Ibid., p. 14.
3. Williamson I, p. 188-189.
4. Ibid., p. 188.
5. Ibid., p. 192.
6. Ibid., p. 191.
7. Ibid., p. 192.
8. Ibid., p. 192-193. In specifically stating that correspondence courses should be developed at the proposed school, Williamson was reaffirming his analysis of the problem of the small library in his "The Need of a Plan For Library Development," wherein he suggested "some care-

fully planned adaptation of the correspondence method of instruction."

9. Williamson II, p. 24.

10. Williamson I, p. 194.

11. Ibid., p. 195.

12. Ibid., p. 191-192.

13. Ibid., p. 228.

14. Ibid., p. 229.

15. Ibid.

16. Ibid., p. 230.

17. Ibid.

18. Ibid., p. 231.

19. Williamson II, p. 70.

20. "The Williamson Report; Comment from the Library Schools," LJ, XLVIII (November 1, 1923), 903.

21. Williamson I, p. 227.

22. "In the Library World: Pennsylvania," LJ, XLVI (October 1, 1921), 807-808. Miss Bogle communicated with C. C. Williamson concerning the need for more library schools and, from the content of her response to his opinion, it appears that he emphasized that the need was for better but not necessarily more library schools. She wrote as follows:
> I agree with you absolutely and I am therefore the more grateful for the frankness with which you have written.
>
> I have been convinced for some years that the only solution for the problem is to strengthen existing schools worthy of so doing, eliminate unworthy ones and surround the establishment of new schools with such care and conditions as may result in standards worthy of professional schools.

Though Williamson's letter to Miss Bogle has not been found, it is clear Miss Bogle wrote in connection with her appointment to the Drexel committee, for she added, "I am using your letter for the information of Miss Rose and Miss Webster as they are on the Committee." Letter from Sarah C. N. Bogle, September 23, 1921. (in the files of C. C. Williamson).

The letter offered to Williamson some indication of the possible reception of his report which as of that date had not been written, by a staff member of the American Library Association. It is possible also that it prompted Williamson to invite Miss Bogle and Carl H. Milam to examine critically the Carnegie report before it was published.

23. "Reopening of Drexel Library School," LJ, XLVII (July, 1922), 614.

24. Ibid., p. 614; ["Drexel Institute Library School" - Editorial comment], LJ, XLVII (May 15, 1922), 466.

25. Williamson II, p. 84.

26. Williamson I, p. 118-120; Williamson II, p. 84-85. June R. Donnelly, former director of Drexel Institute Library School, took issue with Williamson's interpretation regarding the closing of that School and with the letter of Dr. Hollis (Williamson II, p. 84-85) saying that he had missed the point. She offered, in contrast, the following interpretation:
> As he [i.e. Williamson] remarks in a following chapter, a professional school cannot train for any one library; and Drexel never planned to be a feeder simply for Philadelphia libraries. Of the first one hundred and seventy-three students only seventy-six were even from Philadelphia. The policy of the five years 1909-14 was to have free competition, and the best win, no matter whence.
>
> It is not a fact that the Drexel School was discontinued largely on the ground that the demand for its graduates was too slight and salaries were too small to justify it.

"The Williamson Report; Comment from the Library Schools," LJ, XLVIII (November 1, 1923), 904.

27. Williamson I, p. 119-120; Williamson II, p. 85.

In Fulfillment of Objective One					135

28. Williamson I, p. 226.

29. Ibid.

30. Ibid.

31. In thus appraising the facilities of Pittsburgh, Williamson refuted the statement in the catalog of the School which asserted that "Pittsburgh offers unusual advantages as a location for a library school." He rejected the libraries of the University of Pittsburgh and of the Carnegie Institute of Technology as inadequate and noted the lack of special libraries, both professional and commercial, in Pittsburgh. Williamson I, p. 227.

32. Williamson recognized that the Carnegie Library of Pittsburgh, like the Cleveland Public Library, needed "a good training school to select and prepare local people for service on its own staff in clerical and sub-professional positions," but unlike the situation in Cleveland, where the training program was entirely separate from the professional training, in Pittsburgh the Carnegie Library School, with the aid of the staff of the Carnegie Library of Pittsburgh, directed the Apprentice Class. Williamson acknowledged that such a plan might be feasible but warned that "the essentially different functions and methods of the two should be kept clearly in view." Williamson I, p. 228.

33. John Cornelius Christensen presented a financial report on all the departments of the Institute which appeared as a 28-page typed report entitled, Report on a Special Investigation of the Several Departments of the Carnegie Institute, Excluding the Carnegie Institute of Technology, April 29, 1921.

34. "Report of the Survey of Carnegie Institute of Pittsburgh", 1921. (Mimeographed). Williamson's name does not appear on the report itself; it is from the annual report of the Carnegie Institute, 1921, and from the Carnegie Corporation that his connection with the report was clarified. Letter from Florence Anderson, secretary of the Carnegie Corporation of New York, October 3, 1956.

35. "Report of the Survey of Carnegie Institute of Pittsburgh," p. 33.

36. Williamson I, p. 226.

37. Ibid.

38. Williamson II, p. 96.

39. Ibid., p. 92.

40. Ibid., p. 100. Nina C. Brotherton, principal of the Carnegie Library School, did not question Williamson's stated preference for Western Reserve University Library School or the omission of any reference to the Carnegie Library School and its program for children's work from the plan of the future as presented in Williamson II. "The Williamson Report; Comment from the Library Schools," LJ, XLVIII (November 1, 1923), 905-906.

41. Williamson I, p. 223-224. On the basis of his original opinion Williamson, like Johnson, could not have regarded Western Reserve University Library School as one of the better library schools at the time of his study.

42. Ibid., p. 224.

43. Ibid., p. 225.

44. Ibid.

45. Ibid.

46. Ibid. Seemingly aware that he had consistently proclaimed the superiority of Cleveland over Pittsburgh as possessing the essentials for building up a strong professional school, Williamson included the following explanation in the report:
> I regret the more that this is my conclusion, because I am a graduate of Western Reserve University and it may appear to some that I am influenced by that relationship. I have endeavored, however, to interpret the evidence impartially and I am confident that any competent investigator would reach the same conclusion. Ibid., p. 228.

47. Ibid., p. 215.

48. Ibid., p. 216. Williamson stated later that librarians and heads of departments in libraries in cities such as Atlanta and Savannah should not only be graduates of professional library schools, they should also be college gradu-

In Fulfillment of Objective One   137

ates and that even that need was not being met by the Atlanta School. Ibid., p. 221.

49.   Ibid., p. 217.

50.   Ibid.

51.   Ibid.

52.   Ibid., p. 221.

53.   Ibid., p. 218.

54.   Ibid., p. 219.

55.   Ibid.

56.   Ibid.

57.   Ibid., p. 219-220.

58.   Ibid., p. 219.

59.   Ibid., p. 220.

60.   Ibid., p. 221.

61.   Ibid., p. 222.

62.   Ibid.

63.   Ibid. Williamson defined more specifically the intent of the recommendation in his "Summary of Report," by emphasizing:
> The question of reorganization of the school should be taken up with the Atlanta Public Library. If the library authorities are not prepared to inaugurate radical changes in policy and methods along the lines recommended in this report, the Corporation should seek some other agency through which to work in promoting library progress in the South. It is probable that to conduct an adequate training agency for this large territory a considerably larger amount of money will be required than is now being given to the Atlanta school. Williamson, "Summary of Report," p. 15.

64. "Among Librarians," LJ, XLV (May 1, 1920), 426. Miss Isom had been connected with the library since 1901, was an organizer of the Pacific Northwest Library Association, second vice-president of the American Library Association in 1912-13, and a member of the Oregon State Library Commission. During the war years she had spent six months in organizing libraries in American Hospitals in France and had been director of war work in Oregon and in the five southern counties of Washington. Her loss, an immeasurable one, was not lessened by the appointment of a totally inexperienced successor.

For more information on Miss Isom, see Bernard Van Horne, "Mary Frances Isom: Creative Pioneer in Library Work in the Northwest," Wilson Library Bulletin, XXXIII (February, 1959), 409-416.

65. Carnegie Corporation of New York, Memorandum, "Appendix F," p. 3.

66. Williamson I, p. 196.

67. Ibid.

68. Ibid., p. 197. Anne Mulheron, Miss Isom's successor, had served as head of the School Department for about one year. Williamson "felt that she is essentially an untried person without special equipment for directing the work of a library school." Ibid.

69. Ibid., p. 201.

70. Ibid., p. 198.

71. Ibid., p. 198-199.

72. Ibid., p. 201.

73. Ibid.

74. Of the Los Angeles School Williamson said: "In my judgment, Los Angeles is the best of the three and has the best location." He also stated: "Even the state of California, with its remarkable interest in libraries does not require three schools." Williamson I, p. 210.

75. For information on the school see R. R. Bowker, "The Riverside Library Service School and its Founder,"

LJ, XLVI (November 1, 1921), 893-895.

76. Williamson I, p. 211-212.

77. Ibid., p. 207-208.

78. Ibid., p. 58; Williamson II, p. 38.

79. Williamson I, p. 208.

80. Ibid., p. 209.

81. Ibid., p. 210.

82. Ibid., p. 211.

83. Ibid.

84. Ibid. To what extent Daniels' disregard of the Association of American Library Schools stimulated a response in Williamson is somewhat conjectural, for his own disregard and low opinion of the Association are thus evidenced in the report:
> Having once recognized without applying proper standards to its charter members, the Association is now helpless, either to enforce the existing inadequate requirements or to make necessary advances. Williamson I, p. 169; Williamson II, p. 121.

In a letter written to Daniels, but not mailed, Williamson did not reveal to his his own opinion, for he wrote:
> It would not be difficult for you to meet the very modest and reasonable standards which the Association of American Library Schools attempts to maintain. Frankly, I must say it would seem to me much better for you to spend your time and energy meeting those standards and getting your school regularly enrolled in the Association.

Letter from C. C. Williamson, March 17, 1921. (Marked "Not sent" in pencil. In the files of Williamson).

85. Williamson I, p. 207.

86. Ibid., p. 212. The phrase "to bring it into cooperative relations with the Los Angeles School" was interpreted in the "Summary of Report" as meaning that the school in the University "should ultimately absorb the Los Angeles School."

Williamson, Summary Report, p. 14.

87. Ibid., p. 213. Williamson was informed by Harold L. Leupp, librarian, University of California, Berkeley, on March 2, 1922, that the University budget for the fiscal year 1922-23 included an appropriation of $6,000 for the Library School. Letter from Harold L. Leupp, March 2, 1922. (in the files of C. C. Williamson).

88. Ibid.

89. Ibid., p. 214.

90. Ibid.

Chapter 5

The Reports of 1921 and 1923

The Report to the Corporation, 1921

The report on "Training for Library Work," submitted to the Carnegie Corporation, was a more comprehensive report than the published version of 1923, since from the latter was deleted all information specifically addressed to the Corporation. The deletions were made upon the recommendation of Williamson because of the confidential nature of the material.[1]

Confidential material. -- The material regarded as confidential consisted largely of the criticisms and recommendations pertaining to schools either receiving or wanting to receive Carnegie funds; it comprised about twenty per cent of the unpublished report. When submitted to the Corporation the report contained the following six chapters which were later omitted:

Chapter	Title	Page
1	Introduction[2]	5-8
20	The Library School Situation in New York City	187-195
21	The Proposed Library School in the Portland (Oregon) Public Library	196-201
22	Library Service for Small Towns and Rural Districts[3]	202-206
23	The Riverside Library Service School	207-214

Chapter	Title	Page
24	The Library School of the Carnegie Library of Atlanta	215-222
25	Other Library Schools	223-231

<u>Other material later deleted.</u> -- Later omitted from the published report were three of the appendices[4] which evidenced Williamson's interest in a certification program; they were:

> Appendix IV Paper entitled "Some Present-Day Aspects of Library Training," containing original proposal for national certification board.
>
> Appendix V Report of the special A. L. A. Committee on Certification, Standardization, and Library Training, 1920.
>
> Appendix VI Report of A. L. A. Committee on National Certification, 1921.

Throughout the report were paragraphs and/or sentences which were also later deleted. The following deletion concerning a librarians' "Who's Who" was deleted possibly because of the reference to certification:

> The acute need of some kind of clearing house of information in regard to persons engaged in professional library work has led to the suggestion of a librarian's 'Who's Who.' If any practicable basis were available for determining what a professional librarian is and who should be included in such a volume, it might do much to aid in solving the placement problem by putting at the service of library administrators and library boards information which they find it difficult to now get in regard to the educational qualifications and professional experience of library workers. The problem of selecting those whose names are to appear in such a guide, however, brings us back once more to the necessity for some certification system for formulating and applying standards for professional library work.[5]

Minor deletions were made throughout the text perhaps because the comments were unflattering or too subjective. Two opinions, for example, one relating to library administrators invited to talk about placement and the other to women graduates, were reconsidered, the former being omitted altogether and the latter, slightly abridged. Of the administrator Williamson had observed the following complacent attitude:

> Impressed by the merits of the school which urges him to become a special lecturer, the prospective employer is likely to seek no further for candidates for positions on his staff. [6]

Concerning women graduates, Williamson attempted to praise the schools for selecting students who would remain in the profession, and, in so doing, he referred to the success of some schools "in imparting to them the kind of training and inspiration which holds them in the ranks of the profession <u>against all other attraction.</u>"[7] (Italics mine). The published report omitted the italicized phrase and thereby removed the only slightly humorous touch in the entire report, for on the basis of the original statement, Simmons College, with the highest percentage of women graduates who had married--27.5 per cent--could well have been chided. [8]

The significance of the unpublished report lay, however, not in the minor deletions but in the specific recommendations made to the Carnegie Corporation, many of which have been referred to in the preceding sections but which have not been viewed in formal array. Williamson's own summary of the recommendations contributes, therefore, to identifying the differences between the reports of 1921 and 1923.

"Summary of Report" Prepared for the Trustees

At the request of James Bertram, Williamson prepared, not, according to him, a summary, but a guide of seventeen pages incorporating briefly the recommendations which he had proposed. In contrast, he made minimal references to his findings having to do with the organization and administration of the library schools themselves, such as curriculum, entrance requirements, teaching staff, methods of instruction, the professional library school and the university, specialized courses, placement of graduates, correspondence instruction and certification. In a preliminary statement he referred to Carnegie's personal interest in libraries, the resultant opinions held that the Corporation was looked upon as having occupied the library field, and informed the Corporation that

> Everyone with the library problem at heart cherishes the hope that the Corporation will continue to devote at least a small share of its resources to the library cause, for the reason, in the first place, that it seems to offer a larger return for the investment than any other form of educational work; and, in the second place, because, if the Corporation, having once occupied the field (as is commonly assumed) should now completely abandon it, the damage to library progress would be irreparable. 9

Williamson carefully delineated eight recommendations, not one of which cited definite sums of money, but all of which involved action on the part of the Corporation. Of the eight, only one related indirectly to library training, that being the recommendation pertaining to the improvement of library service in small towns and rural districts through the development of the concept of the county library system. Four related to specific schools surveyed and three to the improvement of training in general by proposing

(1) that funds be allocated for the preparation of text-books; (2) that fellowships and scholarships be awarded by the Corporation on a competitive basis to college men and women; (3) that support be given to a plan of certification and accreditation should such a plan receive the endorsement of the library profession.

Of the eight recommendations, only the one referring to financial aid for a certification and accrediting program had not been clearly stated in the original report. Williamson's emphasis, however, on the plan's being presented with the endorsement of the library profession definitely placed the initiative for the fulfillment of the recommendation on the profession; therefore only seven of the recommendations were to be acted upon by the Corporation.

As a final recommendation, Williamson, aware that should the recommendations be implemented "continuous expert attention" would be essential, suggested that the Corporation might perhaps (1) implement some of the recommendations through the American Library Association; (2) handle the work within its own staff; (3) establish an agency for the implementation of the recommendations and for constant survey of library problems. It was the last of the suggestions that Williamson endorsed, however, because of his recognition that no existing agency was prepared to execute all the recommendations contained within his study, "Training for Library Work."

The "Summary" concluded with a brief reference to "other problems proposed for study." They were: (1) library service and library training for Negroes; (2) library service for the foreign born; (3) the public library's need for professional and lay groups interested in its developments and improvement.

In the following pages the "Summary of Report" will be transcribed in full from the carbon copy in the possession of C. C. Williamson before his death.

Summary of Report
on
Training for Library Work
Prepared for the
CARNEGIE CORPORATION OF NEW YORK
by
C. C. Williamson
1921

NOTE: The principal recommendations involving action on the part of the Corporation are indicated by underscored passages in Sections 9, 16, 18, 19, 20, 22, 23, and 24.

1. This investigation was begun with the understanding that the Corporation desired an objective study of library schools and other training agencies in their relation to the need for a trained personnel in library service, in order to have available all the information necessary for the consideration of any particular proposal in the library field that might come up for consideration. Consequently, the report as submitted is not primarily of the nature of a program which the Corporation might follow if it should desire to take a hand in improving training for library service. At various points, however, it seemed desirable to call attention incidentally to what seemed to the writer to be special opportunities for the Carnegie Corporation, or some other philanthropic body, to take a helpful part in initiating or stimulating progressive measures. It also seemed necessary to report specifically, with recommendations, on several library schools which have or desire to have financial aid from the Corporation.

On reading the report Mr. Bertram felt it would add to its value to have it supplemented by a brief summary of the recommendations. The following paragraphs have been written for this purpose. In a sense they should not be called a summary of the report, for an adequate statement of the findings cannot be made in so brief a form. They may, however, serve as a guide to the report, so far as it attempts to suggest ways in which the Corporation might be of assistance.

The conclusions and recommendations having to do with the organization and administration of library schools, being of primary interest only to librarians and to the schools themselves, are touched upon very lightly in this summary. It may be desirable, however, for the Corporation to ask the library schools to consider these recommendations and be guided by them as a condition of receiving financial support.

2. Before taking up the report itself the writer wishes to take the liberty of pointing out one of the reasons why it would seem to him to be a wise policy for the Carnegie Corporation to adopt a program of aiding in the promotion of public library service through training and other practicable methods. No general discussion of the pros and

cons of such a course will be undertaken; it is desired merely to emphasize this one point.

From his somewhat limited knowledge of the programs and policies of the great philanthropic foundations it has seemed to the writer that the important fields of endeavor open to them are rather narrowly limited by political or other practical considerations. Newer organizations seem to be having difficulty in finding a special field not already preempted in which there is an obvious opportunity for private philanthropy to do constructive work of lasting and far-reaching character. This difficulty will probably become more acute as time goes on and the number of endowed agencies increases.

Within certain limits, not yet sufficiently well defined, it seems that the promotion of library service, particularly that of general public libraries, offers as attractive and fruitful a field as can be found in the whole range of education and social welfare. It is practically virgin soil. Aside from buildings and an occasional endowment, little thought or money has been put into the development of this agency of community and individual welfare. It is possible, moreover, that buildings and endowments are among the least desirable forms for private philanthropy to take. Some phases of this question were discussed by the writer in an address on Mr. Carnegie's library philanthropies delivered to the Western Reserve University Library School, which is available in print and can therefore be merely referred to here.

As a result of Mr. Carnegie's personal interest in libraries, the Carnegie Corporation has come to be looked upon as having definitely occupied the library field. Other foundations will hesitate for a long time to enter it, or even to consider it, taking the attitude naturally enough that the Carnegie Corporation is in a position to do anything that needs to be done or is worth doing. Everyone with the library problem at heart cherishes the hope that the Corporation will continue to devote at least a small share of its resources to the library cause, for the reason, in the first place, that it seems to offer a larger return for the investment than any other form of educational work; and, in the second place, because, if the Corporation, having once occupied the field (as is commonly assumed) should now completely abandon it, the damage to library progress would be irreparable.

3. General statement in regard to the report. --
The report submitted and approved by the Advisory Committee, containing about 100,000 words, is primarily a survey of the existing library schools, with incidental discussion of other types of training agencies. The schools are subjected to a statistical and critical examination resulting in chapters on the curriculum, entrance requirements, teaching staff, methods of instruction, finances, need of specialized courses, correspondence instruction, and certification. Special reports are made on certain library schools which have received financial aid from Mr. Carnegie or the Carnegie Corporation or are seeking support from the Corporation.

An effort has been made to detect and point out the strong and weak points in the organization of the library schools and the training which they offer. Many of the defects disclosed could be remedied by the schools themselves; others are due to their extreme poverty and can only be removed by larger incomes.

4. How the survey was made. -- In the preparation of the report all existing sources of information were examined and numerous conferences held with individuals and groups interested in the training problem. During the latter part of 1920 and the early part of 1921 each of the library schools which claims to give at least one academic year of instruction was visited. Personal inspection of plant and equipment and consultation with principals and faculties were followed up by questionnaires and correspondence.

5. Curriculum. -- An analysis of the curricula of the schools shows a wide variation in the time devoted even to the most important subjects, which suggests the desirability of working out standard minimum essentials for each important course (p. 37), as well as some degree of uniformity in the terminology used to describe the curriculum. Too much emphasis is laid, both in entrance requirements and in the curriculum, on pure literature, to the neglect of the literature of technical, business, social, economic, and political subjects.

6. Entrance requirements. -- Only two of the library schools require college education for admission. While a considerable proportion of the students in the other schools have had a college course, a high school education

The Reports of 1921 and 1923   151

is still the minimum requirement. Throughout the report
reasons are set forth for believing that the time has come
to demand a well-balanced college course as the educational
basis for professional training for library work. Critical
examination of entrance examinations (p. 43-45), "personality
tests", and other features of the present admission requirements should lead the schools to modify their present methods.

      7. The teaching staff. -- An effort should be made
at once to improve the quality of instruction in the library
schools. A study of the training and experience of members
of the teaching staffs (p. 55-59) indicates a low standard.
Less than half of the instructors are college graduates.
Forty-two per cent are teaching in the same school in which
they received their own technical training. Only a small
percentage have had any training or experience in teaching
and about one-third have taken up the work without adequate
professional experience.

      While the causes for this condition are somewhat
complex, it is believed that low salaries are at the root of
the difficulty. The best paid instructors, aside from the
principals, receive about $2,000 a year, which is little more
than the initial salary of graduates of the best schools at
the present time.

      8. Methods of Instruction. -- The outstanding con-
clusion in regard to methods of instruction is that the lecture
system is used to excess, due to poor preparation, overwork,
and lack of skill on the part of the teacher, and inadequate
or uneven preparation on the part of the students. The poor
teaching in general is rendered still worse by a system of
part-time instruction made necessary by lack of money to
pay salaries (p. 60-69).

      "Field work" as a part of the library school course
was thoroughly studied (p. 76-95). While it seems that
many of the defects disclosed might be removed by the
schools themselves, it is apparent that they are helpless to
remedy the fundamental fault, namely, a lack of funds
necessary to employ more competent supervisors of field
work.

      9. Text-Books. -- The lack of suitable text-books
and adequate handbooks and treatises covering the important
phases of library administration and practice constitutes a

serious handicap for the library schools. Such books are not published because those who could write them are not able to find the time while carrying unreasonably heavy teaching schedules. Moreover, the demand for works of this nature would be so small that the author would realize no adequate financial return for the labor put into them. If the books that are needed were once written, however, they would have a large enough sale to meet the cost of publication by the American Library Association's Publishing Board (which was endowed by Mr. Carnegie).

The discussion of the text-book problem (p. 70-75) closes with the following recommendation: <u>A very important contribution could be made at this time to the improvement of instruction in library schools by a comparatively small amount of money used to stimulate the preparation of textbooks and manuals adapted for instructional purposes. It is recommended that the Carnegie Corporation appropriate for a period of five years a sum of money large enough to pay the salary, and perhaps allow something for traveling expenses, of one library school instructor on leave of absence each year for the specific purpose of enabling him to complete for publication a work which when published will be useful to the schools and to the library profession generally. Such a prize or fellowship should be made competitive and awarded by a properly constituted committee instructed to select the person who has in hand the piece of work most needed by the schools and so near completion that it can be finished within the year.</u>

10. <u>The professional library school and the university.</u> -- One of the most important conclusions of the study is that professional library schools should not be conducted by public libraries, state or municipal, but should be organized as a part of a university, along with other professional schools of the better class (p. 122-126). Schools now conducted by public libraries should be transferred to university auspices as rapidly as practicable and no more established. Public libraries will still need to conduct their own training classes, but should no longer attempt to organize professional schools. This conclusion is based primarily on considerations of educational policy, but also on the ground of the fiscal impropriety of supporting general professional training from local municipal funds. Under proper university auspices higher standards for the teaching staff and more adequate educational standards for students may be anticipated.

The Reports of 1921 and 1923   153

   11. <u>Finances</u>. -- Library schools are conducted on
wholly inadequate financial basis. Only four schools have
an income in excess of $10,000 a year. While very few
schools have an independent financial status, it appears from
information secured that their resources have not been keeping pace with the needs of library service or with other
professional training agencies (p. 100-105).

   12. <u>Statistics of students and graduates</u>. -- In the
year 1920-1921 about 371 students were enrolled in the
fifteen schools--a number which represents approximately
60 per cent of their total physical capacity. This and
other considerations suggest that the pressing need is not
the establishment of additional library schools, but for
strengthening existing schools and operating them to something like their full capacity (p. 104-108).

   About 5,000 graduates in all have been sent out by
the fifteen schools, of which 62 per cent are still actively
engaged in library work. Less than 6 per cent of the total
number of graduates were men. One of the conclusions of
the study is that to attract the larger number of men needed
in library service, the schools should be put on a graduate
basis with higher professional standards.

   13. <u>Salaries of graduates</u>. -- An analysis of the
salaries of the graduates of five representative schools
(p. 100-116) shows that over 40 per cent earn less than
$1,500 a year; only 15 per cent as much as $2,000 a year;
and only 3.6 per cent as much as $2,500 a year. A chap-
ter (p. 117-120) on "The relation of salaries to improvement
of library schools" points to the conclusion that higher professional standards, with more adequate compensation, must
go hand in hand with the improvement of library schools.

   14. <u>Specialized courses</u>. -- One of the main criticisms of existing library schools is their failure to provide
specialized training. While library service has become
highly specialized, the professional schools, with very few
exceptions, continue to give only a brief general course.
The report holds that while a one-year course can be made
adequate for the general professional training, a second
year of specialized study should be offered. A definite plan
is outlined (p. 127-142) for the development of specialized
training at a minimum of expense.

   15. <u>Placement of graduates</u>. -- Library schools are

placement as well as training agencies. The reason for
this conspicuous fact and its significance are commented
upon (p. 143-146) and certain suggestions offered as to the
acute need for some clearing house of information in regard
to persons engaged in library work.

      16. <u>Fellowships and scholarships.</u> -- One recommendation growing out of the survey of the Carnegie Library
School of Atlanta is that the <u>Carnegie Corporation should
provide scholarships in northern library schools for young
women from southern states</u> (p. 222). Such scholarships
awarded to educated southern women on a competitive basis
and on condition that they take up library work in their own
states, could be made a very potent means for developing
leadership and public interest in the more backward states.

      A chapter on the so-called "recruiting problem",
occasioned by the apparent shortage of library workers and
a reduced enrolment in the library schools, also leads to
the recommendation (p. 153) that the <u>Carnegie Corporation
establish a few competitive scholarships in one or more of
the best library schools to stimulate the recruiting of library
school classes from among the most promising college
graduates.</u>

      17. <u>Correspondence instruction.</u> -- Throughout the
study and report much attention has been given to the need
and possibilities of professional improvement of library
workers while in service. A special chapter (p. 154-158)
on "Training in service", reviewing the agencies and methods
which have been used, is followed by a chapter on "Correspondence instruction" (p. 159-167) in which the present
status of instruction by mail is outlined and its applicability
to library work discussed. The conclusion is that the
correspondence method, which has scarcely been tried in
the library field, holds large possibilities both for general
elementary training and graduate specialized study, if conducted under proper conditions; that no existing agency is in
a position to develop the work; and that the reorganized library school proposed for New York City should be expected
to take it up and make a thorough demonstration (p. 193).

      18. <u>Certification.</u> -- Fundamental to the problem of
raising standards of professional training is the need for a
system of professional certificates and some properly constituted body for accrediting training agencies. One of the
earliest and most important conclusions reached in the study

The Reports of 1921 and 1923   155

was the need for some national certifying and accrediting
authority. The value and possible functions of a national
certification board are pointed out throughout the report.
An entire chapter (p. 168-180) and a long appendix (p. 249-
276) are devoted to a detailed study of the certification
problem, with specific recommendations. The project in its
present form contemplates action on the part of the American
Library Association - action which has not yet been taken,
due largely to a certain feeling of apprehension on the part
of state library authorities that national standards may gain
so much prestige as to interfere with state and local auton-
omy.

Principals of most library schools and most of the
leading librarians are strongly in favor of the creation of
some central body for supervising and accrediting library
schools and other training agencies. This report when published should be of great assistance in crystallizing sentiment
in favor of such a standardizing body. When the time is
ripe to launch it, financial support will be needed. <u>It is
recommended that the Carnegie Corporation should be ready
to give its aid whenever a concrete proposal is presented
with the endorsement of the library profession.</u>

19. <u>Trained personnel for the small library.</u> -- One
of the problems constantly kept in mind in the preparation of
the report is the need for improvement of library service in
small towns and rural districts, which means, in other words,
in the hundreds of communities which have a Carnegie library building but no adequate library service. It is believed
(See p. 181-186) that the amount of improvement it is possible
to effect by the stimulation of training adapted specifically to
the type of librarian and the economic situation represented
by the small independent public library is very narrowly
limited. The system of small isolated, independent library
units is believed to be fundamentally unsound. The primary
effort should therefore be devoted to the promotion of the
so-called county system. General improvement in standards
of professional qualifications and training through certification and better library schools can be relied upon to accomplish more for the small community than the multiplication
of summer schools and library schools of the usual type.

The county library system has reached a high state
of development in California and Oregon. But the idea
spreads slowly, being impeded to some extent by the existence of the many small Carnegie library buildings. <u>It is</u>

therefore recommended (p. 205-206) that the Carnegie Corporation adopt two methods of improving library service in small towns: (1) cause a careful study to be made of the county library system as it operates in California and elsewhere and publish a semi-popular report which would serve to spread the idea of the county system; (2) follow up the study and report by establishing and maintaining demonstration county libraries, or model experimental units. The aim should be to give the counties selected the best possible library service without spending more money than they could be expected eventually to spend for that service from their own resources, to try out various methods and to report fully and continuously in such a way as to popularize the county system and create a demand for it throughout the country. These demonstration units would also serve the important purpose of providing suitable places for observation and practice for students taking special training for service in county systems.

In the meantime, while the county system is being developed and leaders trained in better library schools, some improvement can be effected through indirect assistance to state library commissions and other agencies conducting summer schools, as well as through the system of correspondence instruction recommended.

20. The library school in New York City. -- A special study was made (p. 187-195) of the library school situation in New York City, with reference to the continued support of the Library School of the New York Public Library by the Corporation. In 1911 Mr. Carnegie agreed to contribute $15,000 a year for five years to enable the New York Public Library to conduct a library school. Since the expiration of the five-year pledge the Carnegie Corporation has continued the donation, increasing it to $20,000 for the school year 1921-1922.

While it is pointed out that this school has made a creditable record and is worthy of continued and enlarged support, the question is raised as to whether the time has not come to effect a reorganization which will enable this school to take full advantage of the unique opportunity presented to a professional library school in New York City. In line with the general conclusion of the study that professional library schools should be organized within the universities it is recommended that this school be transferred to Columbia University and adequately endowed.

This recommendation is based on the belief that training for library work in general can better be promoted by establishing one strong school than by making small grants to several schools. One first-class school in New York City would be able to set standards which others would have to meet. It would help to discourage the unfortunate tendency to start library schools in public and university libraries without proper personnel or financial support.

The proposed school would be expected to lead the way in developing the kind of specialized courses advocated in this report. It should offer training for those who are to teach in other library schools and in training classes. This school would be expected to develop and carry on the country-wide system of correspondence instruction discussed and recommended elsewhere. It is further recommended that a library information service be conducted in connection with this school, giving the members of the teaching staff constant contact with actual library problems, providing fresh teaching material, and affording opportunities for the making of field studies which would be invaluable both to the faculty and to the advanced students. A permanent exhibit of library equipment and methods might also be found of great utility.

Without going into greater detail here, it may be said that this school would be expected to assume a position of leadership in raising standards of professional training in the various ways pointed out in the report as desirable.

21. Proposed library school in the Portland (Oregon) Public Library. -- A project for the establishment of a library school in the public library of Portland, Oregon, for which funds had been sought from the Carnegie Corporation, was investigated (p. 196-201). The conclusion reached is that it would be unwise for the Corporation to subsidize or endow a library school in Portland at the present time. This opinion is based mainly on the lack of a strong personnel and a satisfactory university affiliation. There is also a serious question as to the need for a professional library school in Oregon at this time. When it becomes clear that a school is needed and the state of Oregon or the City of Portland is prepared to contribute the larger share of the cost of running a first-class school, it may be in order for the Carnegie Corporation to consider a request for financial assistance.

22. Riverside Library Service School and the situation in California. -- The Riverside Library Service School has hoped to receive support, probably in the form of endowment, from the Carnegie Corporation. The survey of this school and the general situation in California (p. 207-214) shows clearly that it would not be advisable to put any money into this school under present conditions. This is the weakest of the three schools in the state and does not have a satisfactory location for a first-class professional school. The existing school has the enthusiastic moral support of the local community, which apparently sees in it a means of advertising Riverside. Outside of Riverside it is difficult to find any qualified opinion in the state in favor of its continuation.

It is believed that all the efforts toward improving library training in the state should be put into the development of the two strategically located schools at Berkeley and Los Angeles - the former a part of the state university and the latter supported by the public library of Los Angeles. If the Corporation is prepared to aid library training in any way in California, it could apparently do nothing more useful than to offer temporary assistance to the school in the state university, which should ultimately absorb the Los Angeles school. An opportunity seems to be offered here to set a stimulating example of what a library school in a state university should be. With a little temporary help it is possible that this state school might become the western counterpart of the leading school recommended for Columbia University. This suggestion is repeated here without knowledge of the latest development in securing an adequate state appropriation for the school at Berkeley and with no intimation as to whether the assistance of the Corporation would be acceptable in any case.

23. The Library School of the Carnegie Library of Atlanta. -- In 1905 a library school was established in the Carnegie Library of Atlanta by means of a special donation from Mr. Carnegie. Since that time annual contributions by Mr. Carnegie or the Carnegie Corporation have amounted to about $75,000, the present annual subsidy being $4,500. The question has been raised as to whether money given to this school is yielding an adequate return in the way of training for librarianship in the South. The first-hand study which was made of the school for this report indicates that it is not doing all that might or should be done to meet the urgent needs of the South. The primary need of the eight or

ten states regarded as the field of the Atlanta school is for efficient agencies for training in service, to reach the untrained and often uneducated librarian who can by no possibility pass the entrance examinations, or afford the time and expense necessary to take the one-year course in residence in the Atlanta school. The school is attempting without adequate income or equipment, to follow the methods and nominally adhere to the standards obtaining in the professional schools of the northern states which have a very different problem to meet.

In the judgment of the writer, the Atlanta Library School should cease to imitate northern schools and organize to meet the special conditions in the South. Instead of eight students per year, few of whom go into the smaller public libraries of the South or remain in them, the school should reach out a helping hand to the scores of librarians who would benefit by short intensive courses.

The question of reorganization of the school should be taken up with the Atlanta Public Library. If the library authorities are not prepared to inaugurate radical changes in policy and methods along the lines recommended in this report, the Corporation should seek some other agency through which to work in promoting library progress in the South. It is probable that to conduct an adequate training agency for this large territory a considerably larger amount of money will be required than is now being given to the Atlanta school.

24. Western Reserve University Library School. -- The Western Reserve University Library School was started in 1904 with an endowment fund of $100,000 given by Mr. Carnegie. The income of this fund, together with that derived from a tuition fee of $100, is altogether inadequate for this well located and important school. The situation, set forth in some detail in the report (p. 223-225), suggests that the Corporation should take up the question of making a substantial addition to the endowment of this school.

25. Cost in detail of projects recommended not available. -- It is not feasible at this time to specify in detail the amounts of money which would be required to carry out the various recommendations made. It is believed, however, that each proposal is outlined with sufficient definiteness to indicate the approximate expenditure involved. It is respectfully suggested that the recommendations be con-

sidered first in principle. If the object and method proposed are found to be acceptable, a detailed plan of financing each project can be worked out in cooperation with the agencies which will have to be made responsible for carrying on the work.

26. <u>The Corporation may wish to create a special agency to handle library problems.</u> -- It will be observed at once that none of the recommendations, except perhaps the new library school at Columbia University, calls for any considerable amount of money. It is also evident that there is no central organization to which the Corporation could entrust the execution of the program outlined. Yet if these initial steps in improving standards of training are to be successful, continuous expert attention will be essential. In carrying out certain of the recommendations it is conceivable that the Corporation might work through the American Library Association, but it seems likely that in maturing plans for such work as correspondence instruction, fellowships and scholarships, support of library schools, a new type of library school for the South, and county library demonstrations, etc., the Corporation will find it desirable either to handle the work directly through its own staff or to set up some agency more or less directly under its own control.

The work could be done by the President or the Secretary of the Corporation, or through someone attached to the staff of one of these officers. On the other hand, it might seem better to create some permanent library committee or board, with an executive officer, to make continuous study of library problems, to make recommendations to the Corporation from time to time, and to supervise the execution of plans adopted. The giving of money for the erection of library buildings and the dispensing of large lump sum endowments to institutions presents a comparatively simple task. Any attempt to initiate new lines of work, to study miscellaneous proposals for assistance, and to supervise the execution of plans adopted, will require a kind of service which no existing agency seems to be in a position to give.

27. <u>Other important problems to be studied.</u> -- If the recommendations made in this report or any considerable part of them were adopted, other important opportunities would doubtless follow. For example, since the report was completed the question of library service for Negroes has

come up. It appears that an inquiry is needed to determine what library facilities the Negro population has, particularly in the South, how these facilities can be improved, and what is required in the way of training for colored library workers. Another illustration of problems which the Corporation might wish to have looked into is library service for the foreign-born. Public libraries are recognized as one of the most important Americanization agencies, yet their work suffers a serious and unnecessary handicap through lack of leadership in creating a supply of suitable literature.

Nearly every type of educational agency now has many professional and lay groups devoted to its development. The public library, however, perhaps the most important instrument of adult education, seems to be about the only educational institution still without the sponsorship of a sympathetic, well financed and active organization interested in its development and improvement.

The Report of 1923

A published version of Williamson's report entitled Training for Library Service[10] was made available about four months after the establishment of the Temporary Library Training Board on April 24, 1923, by the American Library Association.[11] According to the introduction, written especially for the published report:

> The primary purpose in preparing the following report was to present existing conditions in this country with respect to training for library work in such a way that the educator and the layman interested in educational problems might be able to form a true conception of the steps that should be taken to improve this phase of the library situation.[12]

Curiously lacking was any reference to the value of the report to librarians and the library schools, yet in the original introduction Williamson had stated:

> The possibility has also been kept in mind that if the report in some form should come to the attention of library school authorities, they may find in it some suggestion or constructive criticism that will bear fruit.[13]

From the published report were omitted all the recommendations included solely for the benefit of the Carnegie Corporation and, as earlier stated, minor alterations were made in the text. Appended to the report was Chapter XIX, "Summary of Findings and Recommendations" which had not appeared in the unpublished report. Before examining that summary some information will be given on: (1) reasons for the delay in the publication of the report; and (2) Williamson's consultation with representatives of the American Library Association. While no formal reference was made to the Association, the report could well have been labeled, "Published with the approval of the Secretary and

The Reports of 1921 and 1923

Assistant Secretary of the American Library Association."
Apparently Williamson himself did not communicate with either of the two groups most concerned with the problems of training, the Committee on Library Training and the Association of American Library Schools or with the Professional Training Section of the American Library Association.

Delay in Publication

Williamson had from the beginning encouraged publication of the report from which the confidential matter had been extracted and was in no way responsible for the delay in the appearance of the published version. William F. Yust, president of the Alumni Association of the New York State Library School, wrote, on May 12, 1923:

> There seems to be something mysterious about this report. It was referred to at last year's meeting of our Alumni Association and again this year. This year some members had seen it.
>
> Will it be possible for me to get a glimpse of it? Wouldn't it be the proper thing to publish this report or make it available in some form so that the library schools concerned could have the benefit of it?[14]

Williamson replied:

> There is absolutely nothing mysterious about the Carnegie Corporation's library school report. The members of your alumni association who have seen it in proof could have told you if they were not trying to make a mystery of it that it [was] being published. It has been in process of publishing for a long time, it is true, but that has apparently been unavoidable. The Corporation has a very small staff and this report has had to wait until other publications were out of the way. They have sent me 76 pages of the proof. I cannot say when it will appear--at the present rate of progress not for a couple of

months.

> Please do what you can to correct the idea that has gotten into the heads of some of the library school people that there is something being held back from them. They won't like it when they get it, but that has had nothing to do with the length of time it has taken to get it published. 15

Advice from the American Library Association

More specifically, Williamson sought advice from Carl Milam, secretary of the American Library Association, and Sarah C. N. Bogle, assistant secretary. There is no evidence that either Milam or Miss Bogle consulted with the officers or the Executive Board of the Association or with the Committee on Library Training concerning the report; rather the two of them proceeded to examine the report critically and to forward their joint opinions to Williamson. According to a letter to Milam, Williamson asked only for his and Miss Bogle's comments, saying:

> The officers of the Corporation have decided to publish it and before putting it into final shape for printing I have wanted very much to have the advantage of such criticism in general and in detail as you and Miss Bogle can give it. 16

The report used by Milam and Miss Bogle was not the full report, however, for the chapters on the special schools had been extracted from it; other confidential matters contained within the body of the paper were retained. 17 Through that confidential material they could have learned that Williamson was suggesting at least two ways in which the schools could be assisted: (1) by financing the writing of proper text-books; and (2) by offering fellowships and scholarships.

Both Milam and Miss Bogle made a thorough exam-

The Reports of 1921 and 1923   165

ination of the report, indicating general approval of content
and specific approval of two basic concepts: (1) that a
college degree should be a prerequisite for admission to
library schools; (2) that library schools should be associated with universities.[18] They agreed, in the main, with
Williamson's statement that

> not more library schools or larger classes, but
> a better grade of student and higher standards
> of instruction are the fundamental needs in professional training for librarianship at the present
> time.[19]

but they were not willing to accept his assumption that existing library schools were properly distributed. Instead they expressed their own belief in the need for an advanced library school in Chicago.[20]

Deletions and minor corrections. -- Some deletions and minor corrections suggested were later incorporated by Williamson--the two deletions previously quoted, and one pertaining to the value of personal interviewing. Deleted from the chapter on "Entrance Requirement," following the statement on the impressionistic method of interviewing,[21] were these sentences:

> Whatever the method of selecting applicants, misfits in library work will occasionally occur. It
> is not apparent that the personal interview does
> anything more than eliminate those who are
> physically unfitted for any kind of library service.[22]

Approval of a plan of scholarships and fellowships was expressed as well as of the comment on the financial support of the activities of professional organizations. The statement, in both the published and unpublished reports, read:

> The possible activities of professional organizations, whether local, state, or national, offer a
> fruitful opportunity for private philanthropy. A
> comparatively small amount of money supple-

mentary to contributions which library workers generally make from their own meagre salaries would accomplish results in strengthening the labors of love which librarians are everywhere giving to their organized efforts. 23

<u>Plans of the American Library Association.</u> -- As if offering evidence of the foresightedness of the Association in anticipating some of the Williamsonian proposals, Miss Bogle and Milam appended to their criticism the following "list of things which ought to be done toward the promotion of libraries and library training" which they had compiled earlier:

Advanced professional training;

Short courses, institutes and correspondence courses for those who cannot take the regular training;

A study of the educational service of the modern library, especially in the field of Adult Education;

A study of the school library movement and its possible future developments;

Reading surveys in typical counties to discover what people read and where they get their reading matter;

Maintenance of model county libraries;

A study of accounting methods, budget making and other administrative questions;

The publication of textbooks on library work, and of indexes and bibliographies needed by librarians;

The appointment of field agents to further the development and extension of libraries, especially in the states without active library commissions, and

The financing of a comprehensive survey of library work in the United States (which has already been started on a voluntary basis by an A. L. A. Committee). 24

Significantly omitted from the projected activities of the American Library Association was any reference to a certification program or to the need of a special agency to improve standards of training. In addition, neither Miss Bogle nor Milam commented directly on certification despite Williamson's reiterative statements. It is possible that their approval of chapter 2, "Types of Library Work" implied some approval for they did agree that "the definitions of this chapter seem to us fundamental,"[25] but they did not refer directly to certification. In contrast, they specifically clarified their views on the need of a second year of specialized training to be completed after at least one year of professional library work, by countering:

> We like the suggestion of a specialized training after the first year, but why limit it to a year? Is it not possible that persons of experience and scholarship will wish to continue their researches along special lines for two or more years, working perhaps for a Doctor's degree?[26]

They presumably ignored, on the other hand, the implications of the following proposition in the same chapter:

> A certification program should recognize the grade of clerical assistant and admit to that grade those whose general education and library training meet the standards provided. Under a certification system which marks the essential distinction between professional and clerical grades, there will be little or no danger that individuals qualified for clerical work will be able to pass themselves off for the higher grade.[27]

<u>Williamson's response.</u> -- On September 6, 1922, Williamson acknowledged his appreciation of Miss Bogle's and Milam's analysis of his report and stated, "I am adopting practically all your suggestions in one form or another." He inquired further concerning the names of other persons who might read the report should the material get into proof,

and asked for names of persons "particularly appropriate" to whom he could submit it.[28]

Readers of the Report in Proof

According to correspondence, fortuitously retained by C. C. Williamson, the following librarians read the report in proof or saw it before it was made available to the public: Andrew Keogh, librarian of Yale University; H. L. Koopman, librarian of Brown University;[29] Judson Toll Jennings, president of the American Library Association, 1923-1924; Adam Strohm, librarian, Detroit Public Library;[30] Ernest J. Reece, principal, New York Public Library School; and William Warner Bishop, librarian, University of Michigan.[31] Presumably many others read the report in proof as the following letter of complaint from James I. Wyer, director, New York State Library School, indicated:

> I wonder whether we can not get hold of your report on library schools. Once or twice before, I think, we have made inquiry only to be told it would be printed some day and that we would then have it. But everyone else seems to have read it or to have a copy. It was discussed at the A. L. A., our graduates write us about having read it or tell us of having seen it, the two faculty members in charge of our spring trip heard of it at different places from people who appear to have read it. It would seem only right that if some of the schools have it all of them should.[32]

Of those definitely known to have read the report before its publication, three were associated with the Temporary Library Training Board, Andrew Keogh, Adam Strohm, who was later made chairman of the Board of Education for Librarianship, and Sarah C. N. Bogle, who acted as secretary of the Temporary Board.[33] Their awareness of and indebtedness to the report was announced in the Sep-

The Reports of 1921 and 1923   169

tember 1, 1923, issue of Library Journal, which indicated that,
at the meetings of May 24 and July 19, before the publication
of the report,
> The Board has devoted itself to the functions
> assigned to it with special consideration to the
> study on library training made by Charles C.
> Williamson, to available criticisms, constructive
> and otherwise, and to such standards for library
> training as have been formulated by the past
> committee on library training and by the Association of American Library Schools. (Italics
> mine.)34

That "special consideration" might well have been
focused on Chapter XIX of the published report, "Summary
of Findings and Recommendations," with a review of the
contents of which this study of the Williamson report will
conclude.

Summary of Findings and Recommendations

Chapter XIX recapitulated the emphases of the report
by synthesizing it into eleven sections: (1) types of library
work and training; (2) the library school curriculum; (3)
entrance requirements; (4) the teaching staff and methods of
instruction; (5) library school finances and salaries; (6) the
need for more library schools and students in training; (7)
the library school and the university; (8) specialized study;
(9) training in service; (10) certification of librarians and
standardization of library schools; (11) the problem of the
small library. The "Summary" contained specific findings
and recommendations which were of significance to librarians
and to the library schools despite the failure of the "Introduction" to identify those two as most likely to implement
the recommendations; from the "Summary" the following has
been extracted:

For the librarians.

Librarians were advised (1) to distinguish between clerical and professional aspects of library work; (2) to adopt a national certification plan which, among other things, would offer an incentive for continued professional growth; (3) to solve the problem of the small library by seeking the extension and improvement of the county library system; (4) to seek to increase salaries and to make library work as desirable a career for men and women as other learned professions.

For the library schools.

Throughout the "Summary" Williamson's basic concepts, motivating the study, were evident; they were: (1) library schools should be associated with universities not public institutions; (2) the college degree should be the minimal entrance requirement; (3) specialized training should be offered after one year of general training and one year of practical work; (4) instruction by correspondence methods should be offered in one school or cooperatively by a number of schools.

Library schools were advised (1) to offer professional training only, leaving clerical instruction to the training classes in libraries; (2) to seek a degree of standardization in the first year of professional training; (3) to abandon entrance examinations and personality tests, admitting on evidence of education and ability to maintain a high standard of scholarship; (4) to improve the quality and efficiency of instruction by increasing full time faculty, raising salaries, preparing textbooks, and re-evaluating the entire program of field work and observation tours; (5) to establish fellowships and scholarships within the university schools.

Published Report and its Reception

The published report, divested of its recommendations, fulfilled only in part objective two of the original study:

The Reports of 1921 and 1923   171

> To improve library service by presenting to the public and to the library profession a clear analysis of the problem of providing an adequately trained personnel for all kinds and grades of library service, and to suggest plans of development to be adopted by public authorities, educational institutions and professional organizations.[35]

Yet its major emphasis was on professional training to be offered, preferably according to Williamson, in library schools located in universities, and on service in public libraries and envisioned county library units. Minimal attention was given to "all kinds and grades of service."

Its sponsorship, however, by the Carnegie Corporation; its belated appearance attended by an increasing curiosity concerning its contents; its publication soon after the American Library Association had established a Temporary Library Training Board which offered partial fulfillment of Williamson's certification program; the publication of chapter XIX, "Summary of Findings and Recommendations," in the September, 1923, Library Journal;[36] and a review of the report in the same issue by Frank K. Walter[37] all contributed to insuring Training for Library Service instant recognition from libraries, the library schools, and the Association.

On April 19, 1924, Frederick P. Keppel, president of the Carnegie Corporation, wrote to Williamson, "Apparently the Williamson report has started something that won't stop in a hurry."[38] What the report started and when, and if, what it started was stopped, are yet to be studied in that period of education for librarianship which may be designated as the post-Williamson period or the post-Temporary Library Training Board period.

Notes

1. Williamson I, p. 6.

2. A brief introduction does appear in the published report but it differs in content from this introduction.

3. In the published report some of the information from this chapter is incorporated into a chapter entitled "The Problem of the Small Library," which was based on the chapter in the unpublished report, "The Problem of Trained Service for the Small Library."

4. The material contained in the three appendices was available in other sources, however, before the publication of the report. Williamson learned from Carl H. Milam, secretary of the American Library Association, that copies of the 1921 report of the Committee on National Certification were available from the Association. Letter from Carl H. Milam, February 8, 1923.

5. Williamson I, p. 148. Some years later Williamson was to edit, with Alice Louise Jewett, a Who's Who in Library Service which was to be published by the H. W. Wilson Company in 1933.

6. Ibid., p. 66. The deletion of the sentence was suggested by Sarah C. N. Bogle and Carl H. Milam who were asked by Williamson to criticize the report. Sarah C. N. Bogle and Carl H. Milam, Notes on Dr. Williamson's "Training for Library Work," September 5, 1922, p. 3. They asked: "I wonder whether the report would not be just as forceful without the last sentence on this page."

7. Ibid., p. 108-109. It is possible that Miss Bogle and Milam were responsible for the deletion, for they noted: "The library school which holds the most of its graduates in the library profession may not deserve any credit for its selection. The fine personality which we want in library work may be just the thing which results in opportunities to leave the profession for service in other fields." Bogle and Milam, op. cit., p. 4.

8. Williamson II, p. 78.

9. Williamson had questioned the wisdom of including in

The Reports of 1921 and 1923   173

the report any reference to the reputation of the Corporation in the library world, but he was advised to retain it by one of the members of the Advisory Committee, Wilson Farrand, who wrote to Williamson:

> I have given considerable thought to the second section, and see no reason why it should do harm and several reasons why it may be distinctly helpful.
>
> Of course the nominal purpose of your investigation was not to advise the Carnegie Corporation in regard to its general policy, but it was clearly understood that one of the purposes was to give it a sound basis for decision as to how it could wisely use part of its funds. There might be objection to your making a public or semi-public statement of this kind, but in a communication which goes directly to the Corporation and is intended solely for its consideration, I can see no possible objection to it; in fact, I should think that it would be welcomed. Letter from Wilson Farrand, March 11, 1922. (in the files of C. C. Williamson)

10. No explanation was offered for the change in title from "Training for Library Work"; however, Williamson had referred to the study as "Training for Library Service" in his "Notes on the Aims, Scope and Method of the Study of Training for Library Service," prepared for the Advisory Committee meeting, April 28, 1920.

The "Foreword" of the published report refers to "training for library service." The "Foreword," signed by Henry S. Pritchett, acting president of the Carnegie Corporation, was actually written by William S. Learned. Letter from C. C. Williamson, February 25, 1957.

11. In establishing the Temporary Library Training Board, the Association had made it possible for the Corporation, should it wish to implement the recommendations of the report, to act upon the recommendation pertaining to the establishment of a standardizing body. The allocation of $10,000 to the Temporary Library Training Board in November, 1923, seems to be a logical implementation of Williamson's original recommendation.

12. Williamson II, p. vii.

13. Williamson I, p. 6.

14. Letter from William F. Yust, May 12, 1923. (in the files of C. C. Williamson).

15. Letter from C. C. Williamson, May 15, 1923. (in the files of C. C. Williamson).

16. Letter from C. C. Williamson, August 18, 1922. Williamson had some acquaintance with Miss Bogle, for he had interviewed her at the Saratoga Conference in 1918 and in 1921 he had corresponded with her concerning the reopening of Drexel Institute Library School.

17. Ibid.

18. Sarah C. N. Bogle and Carl H. Milam, Notes on Dr. Williamson's "Training for Library Work," August 29, 1922, p. 1; p. 5. (in the files of C. C. Williamson).

19. Williamson I, p. 116.

20. Bogle and Milam, op. cit., p. 4.

21. Williamson I, 49; Williamson II, p. 31.

22. Ibid.

23. Ibid., p. 157; Williamson II, p. 112. This reference to "private philanthropy" is the only reference in the published report which could have been interpreted by a discerning reader that Williamson had made recommendations to the Corporation on the opportunities offered for fruitful expenditure of Corporation money.

24. Bogle and Milam, op. cit., p. 8. It appears that Williamson did not incorporate any of their suggestions into the report other than those relating to topics already included, for example, suggestions relating to correspondence instruction, county libraries, and the need of textbooks.

25. Ibid., p. 1.

26. Ibid.

27. Williamson I, p. 20.

The Reports of 1921 and 1923   175

28.   Letter from C. C. Williamson, September 6, 1922.
(in the files of C. C. Williamson).

29.   Letter from H. L. Koopman, March 29, 1923. (in
the files of C. C. Williamson).

30.   Letter from Carl H. Milam, May 9, 1923. (in the files
of C. C. Williamson).

31.   Letter from William Warner Bishop, March 15, 1923.
(in the files of C. C. Williamson).

32.   Letter from James I. Wyer, May 4, 1923.   (in the
files of C. C. Williamson).

33.   "The Library Training Board Meets," LJ, XLVIII
(September 1, 1923), 721.

34.   Ibid.

35.   Williamson, "Notes," p. 3.

36.   C. C. Williamson, "Training for Library Service,"
[An Abridgment of the "Summary of Findings and Recommendations"], LJ, XLVIII (September 1, 1923), 711-714.

37.   Frank K. Walter, "A Dynamic Report," LJ, XLVIII
(September 1, 1923), 709-710.

38.   Letter from Frederick P. Keppel, April 19, 1924.
(in the files of C. C. Williamson).

APPENDICES

Appendix 1

Statement Prepared for the Use of
Miss Sarah K. Vann . . .
June 1955
by Dr. Charles C. Williamson

Appendix 1   179

One of the questions you had in mind to ask me had to do with my reasons for being interested in librarianship. As I said in my letter of May 23, I seem never to have reasoned my way into library work. It came about through a series of unrelated circumstances and events, some of which I will now try to relate to you briefly, so far as my faulty memory permits. Never before have I had occasion to review the various steps which seem, as I now look backward some sixty years, to have added up to a library career, of sorts. I am myself amused by the process as well as the result, but I do not see that it can have any particular bearing on the Carnegie report or any other aspect of your thesis subject. However, the story may possibly serve as a kind of case study in recruitment to the library profession.

I was born and raised on a small farm in northeastern Ohio and attended a one-room country school. My parents themselves had only that kind of country school education and were poor, even by the rural Ohio standards of the 1890's. We had some books in the home, but these were all for adults, none for children or young people, either at home or in the school. (Youth's Companion and St. Nicholas magazine certainly did something to compensate for lack of suitable books.) The school textbooks were pretty dull, though many of the selections in McGuffey's series of readers I found interesting and even exciting. Many of them I still recall vividly. I suppose such reading material would not be tolerated in any present-day school, public or private.

Through some influence which I cannot now trace--it may have been one of the teachers in the country school--I decided one October day when I was nearly seventeen that it would not be worth while to go back to the country school that winter only to go over the same ground I had already covered at least twice before; that instead I would try to gain admission to the graded schools in the nearest town, about three and one-half miles from my home, by unimproved road.

An interview with the pompous Irish superintendent of schools led to admission to an eighth grade class. Though I missed several weeks of the fall term I never missed a day after getting started and had the satisfaction of graduating at the head of the class. Walking those three and one-half miles to school every day in all kinds of weather, winter and summer, would be fatal to most seventeen year olds today, I fear, but I survived it and even enjoyed it except when the snow or mud was knee deep. At all events, I knew well before finishing the eighth grade that I had to go on to high school, located in the same antiquated building, and that I did for four years, graduating as valedictorian.

The high school had no library. Students were not encouraged to read beyond their textbooks and the standard texts in English literature required for admission to college. I judge that our high school teachers had not read much more widely, though they were all college graduates--one a graduate, I think of Trinity College, Cambridge University, England. A real taste for reading was acquired if at all somewhat by accident. And such accidents did happen. I recall one that led to my introduction to Dickens.

The janitor of the old-time school building, the top, or third, floor of which was occupied by the high school (thus literally justifying its name), was a fairly recent graduate of this high school and may have had an unusual home background. In any case he liked to read. I recall

Appendix 1

clearly now, some sixty years later, the day when I stood watching this Mr. Young alternately pulling down and then releasing the rope that rang the large bell in the tower.

How the subject of reading happened to come into our conversation that day I do not know, but he asked me if I had ever read any of Dickens. I had not. He said I should and that he would recommend I begin with <u>Bleak House.</u> I did forthwith, was thrilled by it, and went on to read several more of Dickens' stories at that time.

Many times in these sixty years it has come home to me that the formation of reading habits is apt to be somewhat adventitious in their inception. I would say that in my school days love of reading did not originate very often in the contact between teachers and pupils, and I doubt that it does even today to any great extent. But perhaps the last person to expect a high school student to have as his reading adviser would be the school janitor!

There was no public library in the small town, but during my high school days a group of public spirited citizens, some of them college graduates and others of some cultural pretensions, got together and organized a subscription library. The high school principal and some of the teachers had a hand in it. The fees were no doubt modest enough but, even so, they were out of reach of a poor high school boy. Fortunately some of the teachers found a way to give me the privileges of the library without payment of fees and that meant a great deal to me then and may have had much to do with my later slightly bookish career.

In my spare time I ran a market garden to meet my expenses. What with the school work and the two hours or more a day getting back and forth to school, spare time was spare indeed. But I had summers and weekends and with some help from my father and mother, especially on the marketing end, I did manage to cover expenses and save up a little money toward starting a college course. Even before I finished high school I managed to pass the examinations and get a certificate for teaching in the schools of the county in which I lived. And I did teach one or more summer terms in the ungraded one-room school where I had been a pupil for a period of some ten years, but getting only the education which a child should get in six or seven years at most.

The pitifully small teacher's wages added a little to my savings and in the fall of 1897, with the aid of a scholarship, I entered Ohio Wesleyan University. By waiting on table and tending furnace I managed to finish the freshman year. On the whole it was an unprofitable year. The instruction was mediocre and the courses uninteresting--Latin, Greek, English, and Mathematics, plus military drill which I disliked especially. To gain full freshman standing it was necessary to take an extra course in Latin, three Latin courses in all. The one bright spot that year was the college library. Though I suppose the book collection was only what could have been expected in a small denominational college, it far excelled anything I had ever dreamed of and was housed in what seemed to me a splendid new building. Since I did not care for my courses, I did only enough work on them to get by and then spent the rest of my time in the library reading widely and purposelessly in hitherto unknown subjects and authors. At the end of the year my funds were exhausted and I knew I would never go back to that college.

At this point I believe I made a wise decision. Instead of trying to find a job to earn money for another year

Appendix 1 183

of college somewhere, I decided to study stenography and typing at a local business college. By working on a farm I could earn enough to pay the tuition. At the end of a short summer course I was very far from being a skilled stenographer, but the little skill I had, together with my good record in the high school, brought me the position of assistant to the superintendent of schools. This involved many kinds of clerical work and substitute teaching in every grade from one to eight. It was a strenuous year. For the following year I was made principal of a graded school, teaching the eighth grade, taking the place on her retirement of a much loved teacher who had been in the school system for many years.

As I had to live in town these two years, I was not able to save much money to continue with my college course, but I made much use of the subscription library referred to earlier. The librarian was a cultured, middle-aged maiden lady who had somewhere learned something about cataloging. She had prepared what seemed to all of us a perfect and beautiful card catalog. This is the librarian referred to in my article entitled "Efficiency in Library Management", reprinted from the <u>Library Journal</u> of February, 1919 (p. 6, col. 2). This library was now beginning to take on some of the functions of a public library, at least to the extent of permitting high school students to use it when properly vouched for by the teachers, but the librarian could not bring herself to permit the "unwashed" public to use her beautiful catalog. As an alternative, I was asked to type the entire catalog on 8 1/2 x 11" sheets, making as many carbon copies as I could. How many copies I actually made I cannot recall, but it was the pamphlet catalogue of typed sheets that the public was allowed to use. Of course the mere act of typing from the hand written cards did not make me a cataloger, but it did give me some idea of why and how a catalog is made. (Incidentally, this little membership library eventually became a real public library with a Carnegie building.)

Toward the end of my first year as principal of the Columbia Street school I was offered the position of Secretary to President Charles F. Thwing, of Western Reserve University, Cleveland, with the understanding that I could fit my secretarial work into a full-time program of study in Adelbert College, the undergraduate college for men, the oldest and the key unit in the University. Of course, I accepted, and reported for duty on June 1, 1900.

As this narrative aims only to give the setting for events that seem quite clearly to have been influential in steering me into library work eventually, I pass over everything that happened in the next three years except the influence of the Adelbert College librarian and the establishment of the Western Reserve University Library School.

The librarian was Edward C. Williams. Mr. Williams was a Negro who had graduated from Adelbert College at the head of his class in 1892. Not only in scholarship, but in athletics as well he had made a distinguished record and was perhaps the most popular man in his class. Two years after graduation he was appointed librarian of the College and in the summer of 1895 attended the Amherst summer school of library economy. The year 1899-[19]00 he spent at the New York State Library School, Albany, receiving an honor first-year certificate.

I must have arrived at Adelbert College within a few days of the time Ed Williams got back from Albany with his full credentials as a trained professional librarian. But he

Appendix 1   185

was not a man to flaunt his scholarship or his credentials. He was more likely to conceal them, since he was extremely modest. He was never too busy to go to any length in helping a teacher or a student, or to talk about books and libraries. I made the acquaintance of Williams soon after I began my work in the President's Office and we remained close friends until his death which occurred about December, 1929. (I have at hand no way of verifying that date.) At a Negro Library Conference held at Fiske University, Nashville, November 20-23, I was on the program of the opening session, along with Robert M. Lester, Secretary of the Carnegie Corporation. Miss Sarah C. N. Bogle, Assistant Secretary of the ALA, and Miss Tommie Dora Barker, then ALA Regional Field Agent for the South. My own address was, at the request of President Thomas Elsa Jones, now President of Earlham College, a "Tribute to Edward C. Williams, Librarian of Howard University". I think that address was published somewhere, but I have no copy of the text.

I do not recall that Williams ever spoke of seeing in me a recruit for the library profession. We often talked about reference work which was one of his special interests, and about cataloging and many other aspects of library work, but I think we more often talked about books, new and old. I believe I said in that Fisk University address that Williams had more to do with my eventually going into library work than any other individual.

Before going on with my story I'd like to digress a moment to refer to Mr. Williams' later career. He had married the daughter of the novelist Charles W. Chestnut and was quite well known in Negro intellectual circles. When the Library School was established at Western Reserve

University in 1904 Williams became one of the faculty. But five years later he resigned the Adelbert College librarianship to become principal of the M. Street High School in Washington, D. C. Then in 1916 he was appointed librarian of Howard University. At Howard his librarianship was more or less nominal, because for many years he carried a heavy load of instruction in modern languages. He had a gift for languages and had a speaking knowledge of several and a reading knowledge of many more. Through all this period he was longing to give up the teaching and devote himself to the library. At last that opportunity had seemed to arrive. He had a year's leave of absence at the end of which he was to drop the teaching and give full time to the library. He came to New York to talk with me about how he should spend that precious year. He felt the need of mental and physical refreshment and an opportunity to bring himself up-to-date with library affairs. His idea was to register in the School of Library Service as a candidate for the Master's degree, but I tried to dissuade him from doing that, pointing out that he already knew more in most fields than our instructors and that he should not tie himself down to any schedule. But his wishes prevailed and we accepted him as a candidate for the M. S. degree (which was then our advanced degree). Shortly after the session opened he became ill and returned to Washington where he died a few weeks later of carcinoma.

This brings me to the establishment of the Western Reserve University Library School which opened in the fall of 1904. I do not know now, perhaps never did know, whose idea it was in the beginning to approach Mr. Carnegie for funds to start a library school in Cleveland. I think most likely it was Mr. William H. Brett's idea, but the stimulus

Appendix 1

might have originated with President Thwing himself, or with Linda Eastman, Ed Williams, or Electra VanDoren, of Dayton. Williams was the only library school graduate in the group.

It was probably in the winter or early spring of 1904 that President Thwing arranged for an appointment and went to New York to see Mr. Carnegie. He returned with only a promise that the request would be considered. Some weeks elapsed with no word from New York. Then while President Thwing was absent for several days a letter arrived from Andrew Carnegie--a letter I opened with pent-up excitement. In it were bonds of the American Tobacco Company in an amount sufficient to yield an annual income of some $5,000. (I rely solely on memory for these details.) Dr. Thwing had instructed me to be on the lookout for the letter but not to tell anyone what it contained or even of the receipt of a letter, until his return. I kept the secret, but it was a pretty tough job!

Today it seems inconceivable that any institution would think of launching a new library school with an income of only $5,000, plus tuition fees. But in those days salaries were very low. Even in 1921, as shown in tables published in my report, they were very low as compared with the still modest salaries of today. It was assumed that only two or three full-time staff members would be required and some of the part-time teachers probably received little or no compensation. Although I was thoroughly familiar with the 1904-05 budget, I can now recall no details.

President Thwing himself was active in making plans for organizing a faculty and developing a curriculum for the new school. I was usually present at the many conferences.

From the start Mr. Brett was slated for the deanship. He, with Miss Eastman, Mr. Williams and several others, held many conferences at which I was usually present to take notes and to represent Dr. Thwing when he was absent. The whole process of organizing a new professional school I found very interesting, but I had already made up my mind as to what I wanted to do. Sometime during my second year in Cleveland I had decided after much advice-seeking to prepare myself to teach economics in college.

Although I graduated in June, 1904, I remained at the college as the President's Secretary and Assistant in Economics until February, 1905, when I went to the University of Wisconsin for graduate study in economics. In later years when confronted with the fact that although without library school training myself I presumed to have opinions as to how library schools should be conducted, I sometimes countered, with tongue in cheek, that I had in effect had an informal course at Western Reserve University in the year before that school was formally opened.

Trying to refresh my memory about some of the experiences I am attempting to relate, I have come across a letter I wrote on December 17, 1910, to W. D. Johnston, Librarian of Columbia University, who had asked me to give him a statement of my "training in economics and my library work and interests." I was then in my fourth year of teaching economics and related subjects at Bryn Mawr College. At the time I had no idea why Dr. Johnston had made the inquiry. Later I learned that the New York Public Library had asked Professor E. R. A. Seligman, who had been my major professor at Columbia, and Dr. Johnston to recommend someone to organize a department of economics when the great Astor Library became the Reference Depart-

Appendix 1 189

ment of the New York Public Library and moved into its splendid new building at Fifth Avenue and Forty-second Street later that spring.

In my reply to Dr. Johnston I see that I said: "It was while I was President's Secretary at Western Reserve University that Mr. Carnegie founded the library school. This brought me in touch with many librarians and increased the interest I had had for some time in library work. I read and studied library literature, such as the New York State Library Bulletins, studied various schemes of classification and the methods of cataloging, and also became interested in bibliography and public documents. Most of this library interest was quite outside my college courses and my duties as President's Secretary, and was due in considerable measure to the inspiration of Mr. E. C. Williams, then in charge of the Hatch library."

I will presently quote further from this letter to Dr. Johnston, but to keep matters in proper sequence I may say that about January, 1905, I was offered a scholarship in economics at the University of Wisconsin. Fellows and Scholars at Wisconsin in those days were expected to perform service of some kind in return and my recollection is that they usually gave to the University far more than the value of their stipends. It was nothing short of a system of exploitation of graduate students, an evil that persists to this day in some places. But I did not object to that system for the first year at least. I lived as a member of the family of Professor Richard T. Ely, head of the large department of economics, and one of the best known economists of the day. In this way I was able to meet many interesting people.

To earn my stipend I was to serve as Professor Ely's

personal assistant, and since I was known to have library interests my work tended to center on his large personal library and the economics department of the University library. I carried a full program of courses in history, economics, and political science through the second semester of 1904-05, the 1905 summer session and the following year. When a fellowship was offered me for the year 1906-07 I declined to accept it, because by that time I saw clearly it would take me several years to get my degree under the Wisconsin system of exploiting graduate students who held fellowships. Without consulting Professor Ely or any member of the Wisconsin faculty I applied for a Columbia University fellowship which carried a much larger stipend and required no service in return. Receiving the Columbia fellowship, I came to New York in September, 1906, and by very hard work met the residence requirements, wrote and published a thesis, passed all the examinations and received the degree in June 1907.

Referring to my experience at Madison, I note that this is what I told Dr. Johnston in my letter of December 17, 1910, when events of only four or five years before were much clearer in my memory than they are today. "As assistant to Professor Ely," I said, "I recataloged his private library, or supervised its recataloging, and also classified and cataloged a large collection of pamphlets, clippings, etc. During the last year of my work with Professor Ely I was engaged in collecting books in economics to strengthen the already extensive collections of the University of Wisconsin and the State Historical Society. This gave me greater familiarity with publishers' and book dealers' catalogs and facility in the use of trade bibliography, French and German as well as English."

"At the time I left Madison I was on the point of taking up work with Dr. [Charles] McCarthy, as he advised me to do, and becoming a legislative reference librarian. The Columbia Fellowship, turned me aside from that purpose. When I finished my work at Columbia I had the choice of becoming Executive Secretary of Western Reserve University and Instructor in Political Science, or Reference Librarian in the Cleveland Public Library, or Associate in Economics in Bryn Mawr College. I chose the latter because the Cleveland Public Library position was that of general reference, while I had hoped to specialize, and although Mr. Brett urged the possibility of developing a special reference library I could see no prospect of financial support in Cleveland for the kind of collection I had in mind."

During the four years at Bryn Mawr, handicapped by poor health the first two years and carrying a heavy teaching load throughout, my library interests had little opportunity to be cultivated. However, my study was in the library building and the Librarian, Mary L. Jones, as well as the head cataloger, Mary E. Baker, were among my close friends so that I was able to some extent to keep in touch with library affairs.

With the move to the New York Public Library I felt that I was definitely in my proper element. The library had an excellent professional staff and I was soon able to build up an interesting and worth-while clientele for my department. At the same time that I was organizing my new department Miss Plummer was organizing the New Library School for which Mr. Carnegie had provided the funds. I cooperated with her by giving her students practice work and even gave some lectures to her classes, but I am afraid I always had a rather dim view of the nature and quality of the instruction in that school, including especially my own little part in it. Later I found that the School at the New York Public Library had the reputation of being one of the best in the country.

This narrative may well end at this point. I was now actually a working librarian and taking active part in the work of professional organizations. The move to the Municipal Reference Library in 1914 was not of my own choosing, but Mr. Anderson felt he needed me there, and I have never regretted that move. In many ways it broadened my library interests and helped to prepare me for the various tasks that I was to undertake later.

In a rough way my letter of May 23 takes up where this leaves off.

C. C. Williamson

June 27, 1955

Appendix 2

Extracts from a letter from Dr. Charles C. Williamson, May 23, 1955, addressed to Sarah K. Vann, written in response to a request by Miss Vann for information concerning his involvement in library education in what was identified as the "Dewey to Williamson" period

In the first place, the Carnegie study was completed nearly thirty-five years ago. Once it was completed I turned my attention to other things and have never since given much thought to the early history of education for librarianship, except perhaps briefly when I was editing the volume "School of Library Economy of Columbia College, 1887-1889" (1937) with which you are doubtless familiar.

Many--perhaps most--of the facts surrounding the inception and progress of the study have passed out of my mind and are now beyond recall. I do not think I have ever read the report since the final reading of the proof in 1923. For twenty years I kept in the attic of my house a large box filled with documents and working papers, but in all that time no single occasion ever arose to take a look into that box. Finally, in 1943, when I sold that house and had to dispose of tons of material of all kinds I sorted the material in that box and gave all the printed stuff, largely files of the printed announcements of the various schools up to 1921, to the library schools that needed them. The other materials, apparently no longer of interest to anybody, were destroyed.

Later I did discover one file box that had escaped the fire and I have given it storage room ever since. On receiving your letter I hunted up that box in which there seem to be a few things that may be of interest to you. I will try in the next few days to go through it and pick out such things, and will send them on to you. These are mostly letters related in one way or another to the study. They may suggest to you questions which probably I cannot answer.

You ask for my reasons for being interested in li-

Appendix 2   195

brarianship. I doubt that I ever went through any conscious reasoning process that led me in the direction of library work. It all seems to have come about through a chain of events in which the initiative was not mine, although I suppose at each fork of the road I must have given some thought as to which direction to take. But I doubt that my choices were ever based on adequate information or reasoning.

When I say <u>chain</u> of events, I mean only that one event followed another in a time sequence covering a period of about fifteen years. It seems to me now that no one of these events had any traceable connection with the others. I will try later to conjure up some of the facts about these happenings, but first may I turn to another of your questions?

You are interested in my "purpose in undertaking the Carnegie Survey." My purpose was simply to do a job which the Corporation wanted done, and thought I might be able to do it for them. My contract with the Corporation was mainly through the then Secretary, Mr. James Bertram. So far as I can now recall I had no preconceptions as to what my findings and recommendations might be. I always had a feeling, however, that Mr. Bertram hoped all along I would find no reason to recommend further spending on the part of the Corporation in the field of library training.

I do not have at hand the statistics of Mr. Carnegie's gifts for library buildings, but most of them were in smaller towns. That naturally gave Mr. Carnegie himself, and later his Corporation, a vital interest in small-town libraries. Neither Mr. C. or the Corporation, at least up to Dr. Keppel's time, ever gave money for books or service, just for buildings. There may have been minor exceptions to this rule, though I do not recall any.

Of course not all of the Carnegie buildings were for

small towns, as you will note on examining a list of them. Pittsburgh and the City of Allegheny were naturally exceptions because of Mr. Carnegie's personal and business interests in that community. Library buildings for other large cities probably all could be traced to special personal interests of one kind or another. A personal interest in an individual, or the personal influence of some individual, frequently led him to deviate from the general policies he had laid down for his library gifts.

This was conspicuously true of his gifts for the establishment of library schools. The basis for this statement is the many conversations I had with Mr. Bertram about the four library schools Mr. Carnegie endowed or supported by annual grants. I always got the impression that Mr. Bertram had used his influence with Mr. Carnegie to resist the making of these exceptions to a general policy.

I believe the first such exception in the field of training was the Carnegie Library School, at the Carnegie Library of Pittsburgh, and this exception I would trace to Mr. Carnegie's personal interest and confidence in Mr. E. H. Anderson and personal feeling for the Pittsburgh community. Mr. Anderson had become librarian of the Carnegie Free Library at Braddock, Pa., soon after it was opened and then for nine or ten years was librarian of the Carnegie Library of Pittsburgh. It was during Mr. Anderson's incumbency that the Carnegie Library School was started. During my long association with Mr. Anderson I often heard him speak of his personal relations with Mr. Carnegie.

I think it was Mr. Anderson's influence with Mr. Carnegie that led some eleven years later to the establishment of the Library School at the New York Public Library. Mr. Anderson had become Assistant Director of the N. Y. P. L.

Appendix 2   197

in 1908. For the two years previous he had been Director
of the New York State Library and Library School at Albany.
In view of his relations with Mr. Carnegie and his experience
at Pittsburgh and Albany it was but natural that he should
want a library school at the N. Y. P. L. and that he should
turn to Mr. Carnegie to finance it. His sister-in-law,
Miss Mary W. Plummer, then Principal of the Pratt Institute Library School naturally was his choice for principal
of the new school.

I well remember Mr. Bertram's story of how in
1905 a young, attractive librarian, Miss Anne Wallace,
Librarian of the Carnegie Library of Atlanta, charmed Mr.
Carnegie into giving her money to start the library school
at her library. (Later Miss Wallace, then Mrs. Anne W.
Howland, was Director of the Drexel Institute Library
School.)

From first-hand knowledge I can say that the gift
to start the Western Reserve Library School was extracted
from Mr. Carnegie, doubtless in spite of the influence of
Mr. Bertram, by the persuasive personal solicitation of
two persons, principally Dr. Charles F. Thwing, President
of Western Reserve University, whose secretary I was at
the time. I will say more about this when I tell you of the
various events which I suppose led to my interest in librarianship. The other person was Mr. William H. Brett,
who became the first dean of the W. R. U. school.

When the period for which the subsidies for the
Atlanta and New York Public Library schools expired Mr.
Carnegie personally, and later the Corporation, continued
them from year to year. In the early years of the Corporation I think Mr. Carnegie's personal philanthropies
dominated its policies, but when his death occurred in 1919

the time was ripe for an evaluation of his library buildings program and other giving, and especially such things as library schools, which had been understood all along to be exceptions to a general policy. The schools receiving grants needed more money. Other existing schools were hoping that the exceptions might now become the rule and that funds would be coming their way. Institutions without library schools were also hopefully awaiting an opening to apply for funds.

In my address on Mr. Carnegie at the Western Reserve University Library School, a copy of which I am sending you herewith, I avoided spelling out the fact that support of library schools was not a part of the approved program of the Carnegie Corporation--not yet, certainly. That was not the time or place to dash hopes that were running high.

Another factor had for some time given Mr. Bertram, and probably Mr. Carnegie himself, considerable concern in relation to the amount and quality of service rendered by the numerous small libraries for which buildings had been provided. These building gifts generally stipulated that the community was to provide not less than a certain minimum amount for maintenance of library service. In nearly all cases (actually the word "nearly" can be omitted) that amount was far too little to meet the cost of good service, yet many communities interpreted this requirement as all they could be expected to do. But, worse still, many communities did not even meet their pledge. While Mr. Bertram was always annoyed by such failures he contented himself with getting annual reports. As a matter of fact, there was no way to hold the delinquent libraries to their pledge, even if he had been disposed to try to do so.

Appendix 2   199

But the low standards of service in most of the smaller communities having Carnegie buildings was of serious concern to Mr. Bertram and his advisers. I think probably the main stimulus for my interest in this problem at that particular time came from my many talks with Mr. Bertram.

Early in 1918 I had left my position as librarian of the New York Municipal Reference Library to do research work on an ambitious Americanization Study undertaken by the Carnegie Corporation. My title in that set-up was "statistician". The results of the Study were published in a set of ten volumes. This was not as much of a break with my previous work as it may appear on the surface to have been. I had taken my doctorate in economics and sociology and my library work from 1911 to 1918 had been closely related to various kinds of research in public affairs of one sort or another. A little earlier, at the beginning of World War I, I had taken leave of absence from my library work to serve as statistician for the Federal Reserve Bank's Liberty Loan campaign.

While I am reciting these facts as possibly having some bearing on the questions you ask, I may go on to note that before the Americanization research job at the Carnegie Corporation was completed I was prevailed upon by Mr. Anderson, then Director of the N. Y. P. L., to go back to the position I had had in that library from 1911 to 1914, its scope and responsibilities to be much enlarged. At that juncture he was confronted with a certain personnel crisis to which he felt that my return was the solution. So until the Carnegie study was completed I divided my time between the two jobs, fortunately only two or three blocks apart. The library school study was not undertaken

until I had been back at the N. Y. P. L. full time for a year
or two. (I have forgotten the dates, and they do not matter.)
The field work for the library school study was done
during the winter of 1920-21. Then about June, 1921, that
is before I had got very far with the writing of the report,
I decided to accept a position that had been offered to me
by the Rockefeller Foundation--the position of Director of
Information Service. That involved many things that were
new to me and required study. That delayed the completion
of the report several months. Then after it was completed
the Corporation took much time to make plans for publishing it. Before it finally appeared in 1923, fed by all kinds
of rumors, the library world had become intensely curious
as to what I had said in the report and why the Corporation
had not made it public.

As one grows older he gradually learns that anything
of lasting importance takes time to germinate and develop.
Although the report was finally published about July, 1923,
it was not until February, 1926, that the Corporation and
Columbia University got together on plans for starting a
new library school at the University and I was invited to
organize and direct it. By that time nearly everybody
seemed to be pretty well agreed that my conclusions and
recommendations were reasonably sound. The Corporation
and the University evidently decided that I should be given
a chance to demonstrate that what I had said in the report
should be done actually could be done.

The preceding is set down as a partial answer to
your question as to my "purpose in undertaking the Carnegie
Survey." A part of the answer you may also find in the
three reprints of articles which appeared in the Library
Journal during the period I was working on the Corporation's

Appendix 2

Americanization Study. So far as I can now recall, the main reason for taking up these questions of library training and of the needs of small libraries was the special awareness of these problems I had acquired from my contacts with Mr. Bertram. I suppose it was also the publication of these papers and my contact with the Corporation, as well as my earlier association with the organization of the Western Reserve University Library School, that led to the invitation to give the Founder's Day address in June, 1920.

My association with the organization of the W. R. U. School, just referred to, is rather more pertinent to your question as to my "reasons for being interested in librarianship." But I refrain from trying to go into the answer to that question now. This is already too long to be called a letter. I will endeavor to set down my recollections on this question, and perhaps on the reception and results of the report, within the next two or three weeks. If after you have read all these rambling recollections you think important questions are still unanswered, I shall be glad to make an appointment with you.

Index
(Data in Appendices are not indexed except when
referred to in chapters I-V)

A

Academic and professional courses: combined, Johnson on, 20-21; Williamson's views, 38(n. 63), 107, 108-109
Accrediting body: for library schools and other training agencies, 83, in "Summary," 155; see also Training Board: proposal for
Administrators, library, 143
Admission requirements, see Entrance requirements
Advisory Committee for Williamson's study, 52, 55, 62(n. 26), 75, 79-80
Agency, co-ordinating and controlling, 31-32, 33; see also Accrediting body: for library schools and other training agencies; Special agency
Allegheny (Pa.), library in, 3
American Correspondence School of Librarianship, 100(n. 69)
American Library Association, 50, 160, 162, 164-165; Bertram on, 43; Johnson on, 24, 39(n. 73); plans for promotion of libraries and library training, 166-167; proposal for central body within, for accrediting and supervising, in "Summary," 155; Training Board proposed for, 32, 71-72; Williamson on, 23, 24, 33
Committee on Certification, Standardization and Library Training, text in Williamson I, appendix v
Committee of Five on Standardization, Certification and Library Training, 72, 96-97(n. 32); recommendation for National Board of Certification, 73
Committee on Library Training, 25, 31, 56, 183
Committee on National Certification, 73-75, 81, 82, 87; resignation of Williamson, 75; text of 1921 Report in Williamson, appendix vi
Conferences: and Williamson, of 1918 (Saratoga), 45-50; of 1919 (Asbury Park), 32, 69, 71, 73; of 1921 (Swampscott), 73-74; of 1922 (Detroit), 75
Professional Training Section, 56, 163
Temporary Library Training Board, 162, 168-169, 173(n. 11)
American Library Institute, 43
Anderson, Edwin Hatfield, 11, 46, 53, 54
"Andrew Carnegie: His Contribution to the Public Library Movement" (Williamson), 65-69, 96(n. 21)
Applicants for library positions without training, 67-68
Askew, Sarah B., 49
Association of American Library Schools, 25, 120, 121, 127, 129, 139(n. 84), 163; demonstrably weak agency, 82;

National Certification Board (proposed) to take its place, 82
Atlanta Public Library, see Carnegie Library of Atlanta

B

Baltimore (Md.) library in, 3
Belden, Charles Francis Dorr, 49
Bertram, James, 13, 17, 24-26, 33, 79, 144; and Williamson, 41(n. 97), 42, 44, 45, 52-53, 54; Memorandum Concerning Library Schools, 1918, 13, 25, 26, 42-45, 53
Bibliography: aid of university faculty in teaching, 7
Billings, John S., 11, 36(n. 34)
Bishop, William Warner, 99(n. 53), 168; and Williamson, 99(n. 64)
Bogle, Sarah C. N., 32, 46, 110, 133-134(n. 22), 174(n. 16); and Williamson II, 164-167, 172(n. 6, 7), 174(n. 24)
Bostwick, Arthur E., 96(n. 32)
Braddock (Pa.), library in, 3, 67
Brett, William Howard, 6, 7, 8, 25, 32, 35(n. 24), 35(n. 25), 39(n. 76), 49
Brotherton, Nina C., 136(n. 40)
Brown, Zaidee, 49

C

California State Library, 84
California State University Library School, see California, University of (Berkeley) Library School
California, University of (Berkeley) Library School, 16, 77, 85, 126, 129, 130, 131, 158, in "Summary," 151
California, University of (Los Angeles), 130

Carnegie, Andrew, 1-3, 33(n. 1), 36(n. 34), 144; and Bertram, 42-43; and Dewey, 2-4; and Williamson, 34(n. 11), 96(n. 21)
Carnegie Corporation of New York: and Advisory Committee for Williamson's study, 75, 79-80; Board of Trustees, 12, 52, 59(n. 1); inquiry into subject of schools for training librarians, 1-2, 12, 13-14, 22; involvement with libraries, 16-22, 23, 144; and Johnson Report, 18, 38(n. 55); Keppel on Williamson's study, 171; need of policy in regard to aiding library schools, 14-16; reputation in library world, 148, 172-173(n. 9)
Carnegie Institute of Pittsburgh, 113-114
Carnegie library buildings: and Carnegie, 16-17, 66; Dewey's view, 4, 6; factor in ineffectual service, 65; Johnson's view, 21, 95(n. 8); and library training, 4, 66, 67, 69, 95(n. 8); opiate of self-congratulations, 66; Williamson's view, 34(n. 11), 65-68, 149, 160
Carnegie Library of Atlanta, 1, 10, 137(n. 63)
Carnegie Library of Pittsburgh, 1, 9, 113; Apprentice Class, 113; need of training school, 135(n. 32)
Carnegie Library School of Atlanta, 20, 76, 77, 110, 118-122, 131, 136-137(n. 48), 137(n. 63), in "Summary," 158-159
Carnegie Library School of Pittsburgh, 10, 20, 77, 109, 112-116, 131, 136(n. 40)
Carnegie Library Training School for Children's

Librarians (Pittsburgh),
9; see also Carnegie Library School of Pittsburgh
"Carnegie Schools," 13; evaluations by Johnson and Williamson, 131; see also schools at: Carnegie Library of Atlanta, Carnegie Library of Pittsburgh, New York Public Library, Western Reserve University
Centralization: need for, 70-71
Certain, C. C., 49
Certificate: for clerical and sub-professional class, 87
Certification, 71-72, 78, 81-83, 87, 142, 167, in "Summary," 154; National Board of Certification recommended, 73, 82-83; opposed by Library Workers Association, 97(n. 36); rejected by American Library Association, 74-75; tentative scheme of educational requirements, 73-74
Chicago: need for a library school, 165
Children's librarians: training for, 89, 112, 115-116, 136(n. 40)
Christensen, John Cornelius, 113, 135(n. 33)
Cleveland, 136(n. 46); need for a professional school, 118
Cleveland Plain Dealer, 6
Cleveland Public Library, 117, 135(n. 32)
College education: entrance requirement, 74, 81-82, 91-92, 93, 94, 107, 115, 170
Columbia University, 5, 100 (n. 69), 104-105, 131; in "Summary," 156-157, 158, 160; and Williamson's recommendation, 106
Committee on Library Training, see American Library Association: Committee on Library Training

Committee on National Certification, see American Library Association: Committee on National Certification
Cooperation: need for, see Centralization: need for
Correspondence courses, 7, 30-31, 83-85, 100(n. 69, 70), 132-133(n. 8); at Columbia University, 100(n. 69); at California State Library, 84; at University of Chicago, 84; at proposed Library School in New York City, 84, 132-133(n. 8); at University of Wisconsin, 84; Dewey on, 30; Williamson's recommendation on, 31, 170
Countryman, Gratia, 49
County librarians: training for, 128, 130
County library: demonstration, 130, in "Summary," 156
County library system, 170, in "Summary," 155-156
County library work, 69-71, 85; course offered at University of California, 85; recommendations by Williamson, 85-87
Cubberly, Edward Patterson, 49
Curriculum, in "Summary," 150; at Carnegie Library School of Pittsburgh, 112; proposed for New York City Library School, 105-106; weaknesses cited by Johnson, 20; Williamson's conclusion, 88

D

Daniels, Joseph F., 126, 127, 128, 129, 139(n. 84); see also Riverside (Calif.) Library Service School
Datz, H. R., 47
Davidson, William, 49
Dewey, Melvil, 29, 30, 106;

and Carnegie, 3-5, 6
Directorship of library and library school, 114
Discontinuance of library schools, 111
Donations to libraries: Carnegie policy, 16-17
Donnelly, June R., 109, 134 (n. 26)
Doren, Electra C., 6, 8
Downey, Mary E., 47, 49
Drexel Institute Library School, 109-111, 134(n. 26); Alumnae Association, 110, 136-137(n. 22)
Drexel Library School, see Drexel Institute Library School
Dudgeon, Matthew S., 46, 49

E

Eastman, Linda A., 7, 8, 35 (n. 25), 46, 96-97(n. 32)
Ely, Richard T., 54
Entrance examinations: entrance requirement, 10, 91, 122, 170
Entrance requirements, 74, 81-82, 91-93, 94, 107, 115, 121-122, 170, in "Summary," 150-151; Johnson's view, 20-21
Experience in library work: entrance requirement, 92

F

Faculty: library schools, see Teaching staff: library schools
Farrand, Wilson, 52, 172-173 (n. 9)
Fellowships and scholarships, 1, 164, 165, in "Summary," 154; recommendation by Johnson, 21; recommendation by Williamson, 93, 132, 170; for women in the South, 122
Feminization, 108; see also Women; Women's work

Ferguson, Milton H., 128
Field work, 90, 91, 113, 115, 170, in "Summary," 151
Finances, in "Summary," 153
Financial aid for library training: need for, 64, 69, 87, 95(n. 8), 153
Findley, John H., 49
Foreign born, library service for, in "Summary," 160-161
Foster, John F., 49
Foster, William Trufant, 49
Franks, Robert A., 24

G

Gaylord, H. P., 100(n. 69)
Georgia: librarians in, 136-137(n. 48); libraries in, 118-119
Graduate school: proposal by Williamson, 30
Graduates: comparison of one- and two-year, 89; in "Summary," 153-154; women, 143

H

Hadley, Chalmers, 46, 49
Hamilton, William J., 46
Hasse, Adelaide R., 55
Hazeltine, Mary E., 46
High school education: entrance requirement, 10, 20, 81-82; and technical training, 20-21; recommended for Carnegie Library School of Atlanta, 121-122
Hill, Frank P., 24
Hosic, James Fleming, 49
Howland, Anne Wallace, 10, 110

I

Illinois University Library School, 6, 20, 77, 118
Inquiry into subject of schools for training librarians: plans for, 1-2, 12, 13-14, 22

Instruction: methods, 84, 91, in "Summary," 151
International Correspondence University, 31
Isom, Mary Frances, 15, 49, 123, 125, 138(n. 64)

J

Jennings, Judson Toll, 168
Johnson, Alvin S., 17, 18, 37-38(n. 52), 131; Policy of Donations to Free Public Libraries, 18-24, 44, 95(n. 8)
Johnston, W. D., 55
Josephson, Aksel G. S., 29, 40(n. 89), 47

K

Keogh, Andrew, 168
Keppel, Frederick P., 171
Kirkland, James H., 52
Koopman, H. L., 168

L

Larger units of service, see County library work
League of Library Commissions, 17, 85
Learned, William S., 173(n. 10)
Lester, Robert M., 17, 18
"Letter of Promise," 16, 17, 19
Leupp, Harold L., 128, 149 (n. 87)
Librarians: Bertram's attitude toward, 24-26, 33; Johnson's views, 19, 21; need for qualified and trained, 66; Williamson's views, 27-28, 32-33, 83-84
Library administration, graduate school of: proposed for Columbia University, 105
Library Association of Portland, 15; see also Portland (Ore.) Public Library
Library buildings, see Carnegie library buildings

Library equipment: exhibit suggested, 106
Library handwriting: entrance requirement, 92
"Library information service" proposed, 106
Library institutes, 28, 32, 40(n. 87)
Library schools: capacity of, in relation to number of positions to be filled, 51-52; evaluated by Johnson, 19-20; existing, 50-51, 87-88; identified in Williamson I, 77, 98(n. 48); need for better, not more, 133(n. 22), 165; similarity to training schools, 77-78; visited by Williamson, 77-78; within a library, 114, 116, 125, 131; within a university, 8, 30, 92, 93, 131
Library schools, recommendations for: associated with public institutions, 131; associated with universities, 131
Library training, see Library schools; Training for library work
Library Workers Association, 97(n. 36)
Location of library school: within a library, 114, 116, 125, 131; within a university, 8, 30, 92, 93, 131
"Look Ahead for the Small Library, A" (Williamson), 69
Los Angeles Public Library Library School, 77, 126, 129, 130, 132, 138(n. 74), 139(n. 86), in "Summary," 158

M

Mann, Charles R., 49
Matheson, K. G., 110, 111
Memorandum Concerning Library Schools, 1918

(Bertram), 13, 25, 26, 42-52, 53
Men: excluded from Simmons College Library School, 108; in library schools, 108; make library work desirable for, 170; require schools with higher professional standards, 153; scholarships to college graduates recommended, 132; trained for library work, 94(n. 2), 153
Milam, Carl H., 49, 96-97 (n. 32), 133-134(n. 22); and Williamson II, 164-167, 172(n. 67), 174(n. 24)
Mulheron, Anne, 138(n. 68)
Mysterious report, 163-164

N

National Board of Certification: recommended, 73, 82-83; see also American Library Association: Committee of Five on Standardization, Certification, and Library Training; Committee on Certification, Standardization and Library Training
National Education Association, 56-57
"Need of a Plan for Library Development, The" (Williamson), 26, 27-32, 40 (n. 81), 41(n. 97); comment in Library Journal, 32; discussed by Association of American Library Schools, 32; rebuttal of Johnson's ideas, 23
Negroes: library services for, in "Summary," 160-161
New England: library situation, 106-109
New York City: library situation, 103-106; proposed library school and correspondence courses, 84; recommendation for professional school, 105, 106, in "Summary," 156-157;
training needs cited, 57
New York Public Library Library School, 5, 11-13, 20, 77, 131; affiliation with Columbia University recommended, 104-105, 156
New York State Library School, 6, 20, 53, 64, 76, 77, 94(n. 2)
"Notes on the Aims, Scope and Method of the Study of Training for Library Service" (Williamson), 56-58; hypotheses, 57; scope, original and actual, 56-57, 58-59, 62(n. 28)

O

Objective One (Williamson I and II), 56, 59, 62(n. 28), 103-132
Objective Two (Williamson I), 56, 59; partially fulfilled, 170-171
Observation tours, 170
Ohio Committee on Library Training, 6-7; concepts similar to those of Williamson, 8
Ohio Library Association, 6, 7

P

Pennsylvania: library situation, 109-116; need of library school, 109, 111
Perry, E. R., 49
Personal interview: entrance requirement, 165
Personality test: entrance requirement, 170
"Personnel Specifications for Library Work" (Williamson), 97(n. 36)
Philanthropy: private, 165, 174(n. 23)
Pittsburgh, 135(n. 31), 136(n. 46)
Pittsburgh: Carnegie Library, see Carnegie Library of Pittsburgh
Pittsburgh: Carnegie Library

School, see Carnegie Library School of Pittsburgh
Plummer, Mary Wright, 11, 12, 61(n. 23)
Policy of Donations to Free Public Libraries, Report to Carnegie Corporation of New York on the (Johnson), 18-22, 23, 95(n. 8); not cited by Bertram, 44; recommendations, 21, 34 (n. 10); similarities to Williamson's Report, 23-24; Williamson's evaluation, 23
Portland (Ore.) Public Library, 15; proposed library school, 123-125, 132, in "Summary," 157
Post-graduate course: and Dewey, 29; and Josephson, 29
Pratt Institute School of Library Science, 6, 11, 20, 77
Pritchett, Henry S., 173(n. 10)
Professional associations: support for, 165-166
Public library: and adult education, in "Summary," 161
Putnam, Herbert, 52, 80

R

Rankin, Julia, 10
Rathbone, Josephine L., 46
Readers of Williamson II in proof: 168-169
Recommendations: to Carnegie Corporation of New York from Johnson, 21-22; from Williamson, 69, 144-145, in "Summary," 147-161; for librarians, 170; for library schools, 170
Recruiting for library work, 92-93, in "Summary," 154
Reece, Ernest J., 46, 168
Reference: aid of university faculty in teaching, 7
Reference librarians: best not library school graduates, 90

Report of 1921, see Williamson I
Report of 1923, see Williamson II
Richardson, E. C., 47
Riverside (Calif.) Library Service School, 15, 77, 126-129, 130, 132, in "Summary," 158
Robbins, Mary E., 47
Root, Azariah Smith, 47, 51, 52, 96-97(n. 32), 100(n. 69)
Rose, Grace D., 110, 136-137 (n. 22)
Rowell, Joseph Cummings, 16, 37(n. 45)

S

St. Louis Library School, 76, 77
Salaries: in library schools, 64, 88, 170; of graduates, in "Summary," 153
Sanborn, Henry N., 25, 39 (n. 76), 49
Sawyer, Ethel R., 124, 125
Scholarships and fellowships, see Fellowships and scholarships
Seligman, E. R. A., 55
Service: Bertram on, 22-26; Carnegie's first contribution, 36(n. 34), concern of Carnegie Corporation over, 16-18; emphasis from buildings to, 4, 21, 65-68, 149, 160; Johnson on, 18-19, 22; Williamson on, 27-28, 32-33, 70-71
Severance, Allen D., 7, 35 (n. 25)
Simmons College School of Library Science, 15-16, 20, 76, 77, 106-109, 143; no recommendation from Williamson, 108
Skills: acquisition, 90
Small library, the, 70; Bertram's view on unschooled librarians for, 25-26; concern of Carnegie Cor-

209

poration of New York, 16-18; and the county library concept, 70-71, Johnson's view, 18-22; trained personnel for, in "Summary," 155-156; Williamson's view, 69-71
Smith, Charles Foster, 49
Social studies: in curriculum, 11
"Some Present-Day Aspects of Library Training" (Williamson), 69
South, The: library situation, 120-122
Southern Library School, 10, 36(n. 31), see also Carnegie Library of Atlanta
Spaulding, Forrest B., 100 (n. 69)
Special agency: recommendation for, 167, in "Summary," 160
Specialized courses, in "Summary," 153
Specialized training, 167, 170; for children's work, 89, 115-116, 136(n. 40); for college and university libraries, 90; for high school libraries, 90; for other areas, 90; in second year, 89-91, 115, 116; in second year and after one year of practical work, 170; in "Summary," 153
Standardization: in first year of training, 170
Stearns, Lutie E., 49
Strohm, Adam, 47, 168
Students, in "Summary," 153
"Summary of Report on Training for Library Work." Prepared for the Carnegie Corporation of New York (Williamson), 144-161; text, 147-161
Summer courses, 21; offered at University of Illinois, 118; suggested for Western Reserve University, 117
Summer school programs: inadequate preparation, 7
Syracuse University Library School, 77

T

Teaching staff: library schools, 78, in "Summary," 151; salaries, 64, 68
Text-books, need for, 101 (n. 92), 164, 166; recommendation by Williamson, 84-85, 132, 170, in "Summary," 151-152
Thomas, Dr., 49
Thwing, Charles F., 5, 7, 8
Titcomb, Mary L., 49
Training: secondary to other qualifications, 19
Training Board: proposal for, 32, 71-72
Training class for assistants: recommended for Carnegie Library School of Atlanta, 121
Training class for clericals and sub-professionals: at Cleveland Public Library, 117; in libraries, 170; suggested for Pittsburgh, 114
Training for Library Service, see Williamson II
Training for library work: Bertram's views, 24-26; combined academic and professional courses, 20-21, 38(n. 63), 107, 108-109; Johnson's views, 19-22, 29-32; length of training period and curriculum content, 89; requirements for professional and sub-professional or clerical, 81-82, 87; Williamson's views, 28-30, 65-68, 93-94
"Training for Library Work" (Williamson), see Williamson I
Training programs: weakness cited by Johnson, 20
Two-year program, 89, 105;

New York Public Library
Library School, 11-12;
specialization in second
year, 89-91, 115-116
Tyler, Alice S., 49
"Types of Library Work and
Training" (Williamson),
81-82
Typewriter, use of: entrance
requirement, 92

U

University, the: and the professional library school, 30-31, 170, in "Summary," 152-153
Utley, George B., 46

V

Vocational training: in undergraduate program at Simmons College, 107, 108-109; response from Simmons College, 109

W

Walcott, Charles Doolittle, 49
Wallace, Anne, see Howland, Anne Wallace
Walter, Frank K., 46, 171
Washington University Library School, 77
Watson, William Richard, 46, 49
Webster, Caroline F., 110, 136-137(n. 22)
Wells, Jessie, 49
West Coast: library schools, 123-130
Western Reserve University Library School, 5-9, 77, 89, 115, 116-118, 131, 136(n. 40, 41); committee concerning establishment, 7-8; ignored by Johnson, 20, 131; praised by Williamson, 117, in "Summary," 159
"Who's who," 142, 172(n. 5)
Williams, Edward C., 7, 8, 35(n. 25)
Williamson, Charles Clarence, 12-13, 20, 53-55, 78, 113-114, 179-192, 194-201; and American Library Association, 32, 45-50, 69, 71, 72, 73-74, 75, 82, 155, 164-167, 172(n. 6, 7), 174(n. 24); see also American Library Association and its sub-entries; and Bertram, 41(n. 97), 42, 44, 45, 52-53, 54; "Andrew Carnegie: His Contribution to the Public Library Movement," 65-69, 96(n. 21); appointed to direct Carnegie study, 13, 52; committee suggestions for Carnegie study, 44-45, 47-50; "A Look Ahead for the Small Library," 69
"Memorandum," July 6, 1918, 45-59; "Need of a Plan for Library Development, The," 26, 27-32, 40(n. 81), 41(n. 97); "Notes on the Aims, Scope and Method of the Study of Training for Library Service, 56-58, 62(n. 28); "Personnel Specifications for Library Work," 97(n. 36); "Some Present-Day Aspects of Library Training," 69; and Study of Methods of Americanization, 55, 60-61(n. 22), 69; "Summary of Report on Training for Library Work." Prepared for the Carnegie Corporation of New York, 144-161 (text, 147-161); "Types of Library Work and Training," 81-82; at Western Reserve University, 8-9, 65; see also Western Reserve University Library School
For Williamson's views on and/or involvements with specific topics, see name

of that topic, e.g., Training Board: proposal for; see also names of individuals with whom he was associated or to whom he referred and the names of the schools which he surveyed.

Williamson I: approval by Advisory Committee, 79-80; confidential material deleted, 141-143; preparation and completion, 75-79; scope, original and actual, 56-57, 58-59, 62(n. 28); see also Objective One (Williamson I and II); Objective Two (Williamson I)

Williamson I and II: Titles, 172(n. 10)

Williamson II, 162-171; delay in publication, 163-164; findings and recommendations, 169-170; omissions, 162; reception, 170-171; see also Objective One (Williamson I and II)

Wilson, H.W., 47

Wilson, Louis Round, 49

Windsor, Phineas L., 47, 49, 74

Wisconsin University Library School, 20, 77

Women: graduates, 143; in the South, 119, 122; scholarships for college graduates recommended, 132; scholarships to northern schools for Southern women recommended; and Simmons College, 107, 143

Women's work: library work considered, 92

Wyer, James I., 168

X Y Z

Yust, William F., 64, 100(n. 78), 163